How to DRAW & PAINT
BABY DRAGONS

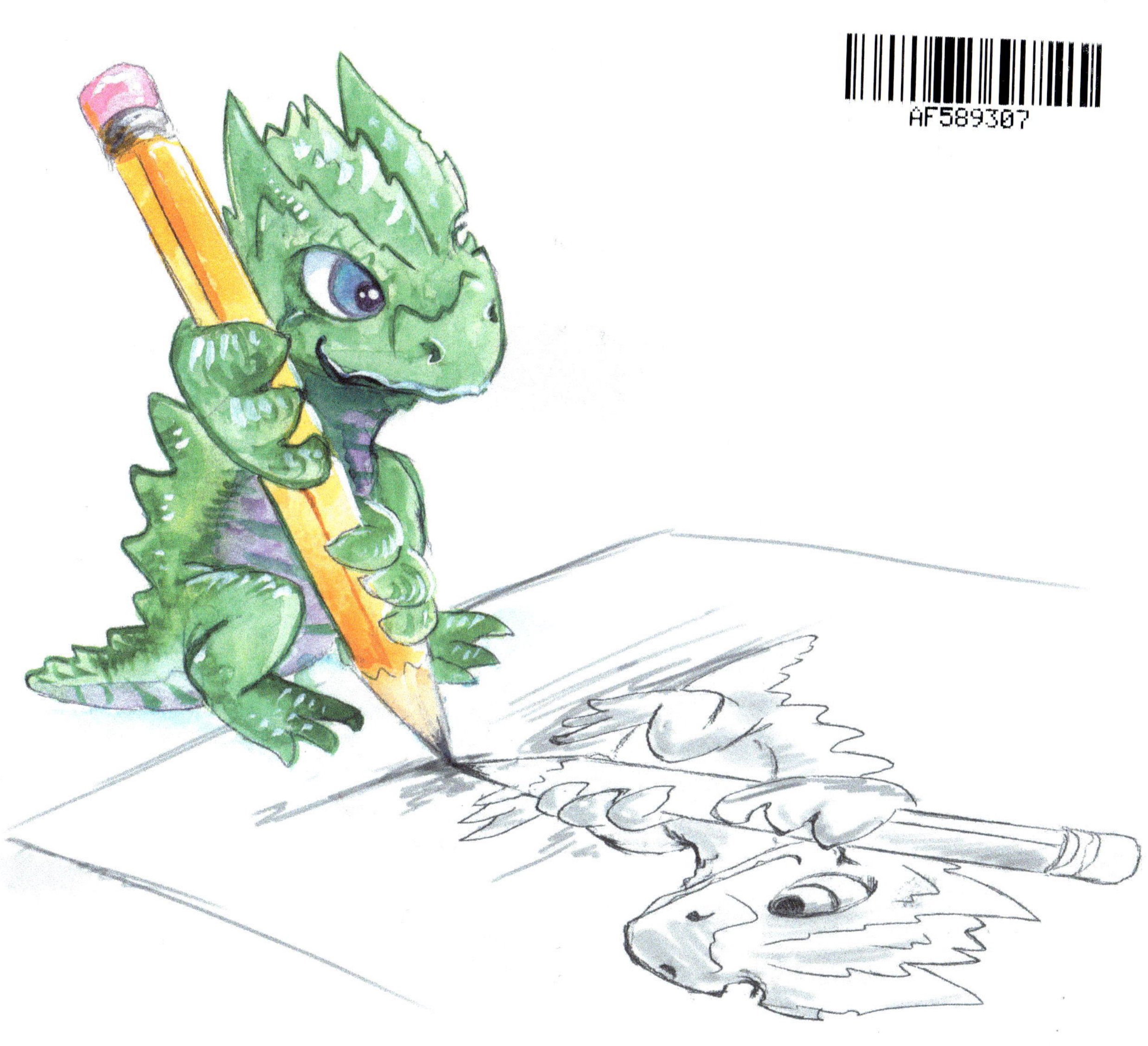

Written and Illustrated
by Jessica Cathryn Feinberg

With special thanks to:

All fans, friends and Kickstarter backers
whose support made this book possible.

To the gang at Maker House for
inspiring and supporting me.

My editor - Victoria Morris
My proofreaders - Janet, Tory & Michelle

FIRST EDITION JANUARY 2015

ISBN: 978-1-942845-88-1

Who can create?

The answer is simple: anyone and everyone can create! In fact, most of us are creative every day in some way or another. It might be the way we talk or dress. It might be something we scribble on a napkin, or in the margin of our homework. It might be writing a letter or planting a garden. Ir might be singing in the shower or dancing in the kitchen.

What matters is this:
EVERYONE IS CREATIVE
and
EVERYONE CREATES
even if we don't realize it.

If there is one thing I've learned in my years of drawing, painting, writing and teaching it is that the biggest obstacle new artists face is themselves. We say you have to be special to make art. We say you have to be talented. We're afraid to try. Trying is scary. The HARDEST part about making art is to get past being afraid of making it. After that you just have to practice if you want to improve. **It's just that simple. Really.**

It doesn't matter how old or young or smart or creative you think you are. What matters is to just do it. Pick up a pencil or pen or brush and do it. It's okay to do it badly at first. That's normal. So let yourself make bad art. Get that out of the way so you can make space for the good art you will be making next.

This book contains some basic tools for drawing baby dragons. The focus is on creating basic shapes and then using them to draw a dragon. You can use these shapes to draw the dragons in the book or as tools to design your own dragons. Remember to have fun and enjoy the process. You will improve with time and practice, but only if you start drawing and keep going even if things don't always turn out right. Have some faith in yourself, keep trying, and remember HAVE FUN!

Now go draw some dragons!

Materials

Each artist has his or her own preference for materials including types of paper, pencils, paint and brushes. Here's a look at the materials I used for the paintings shown in this book. You should explore other materials as well and make up your own mind about what works best for you.

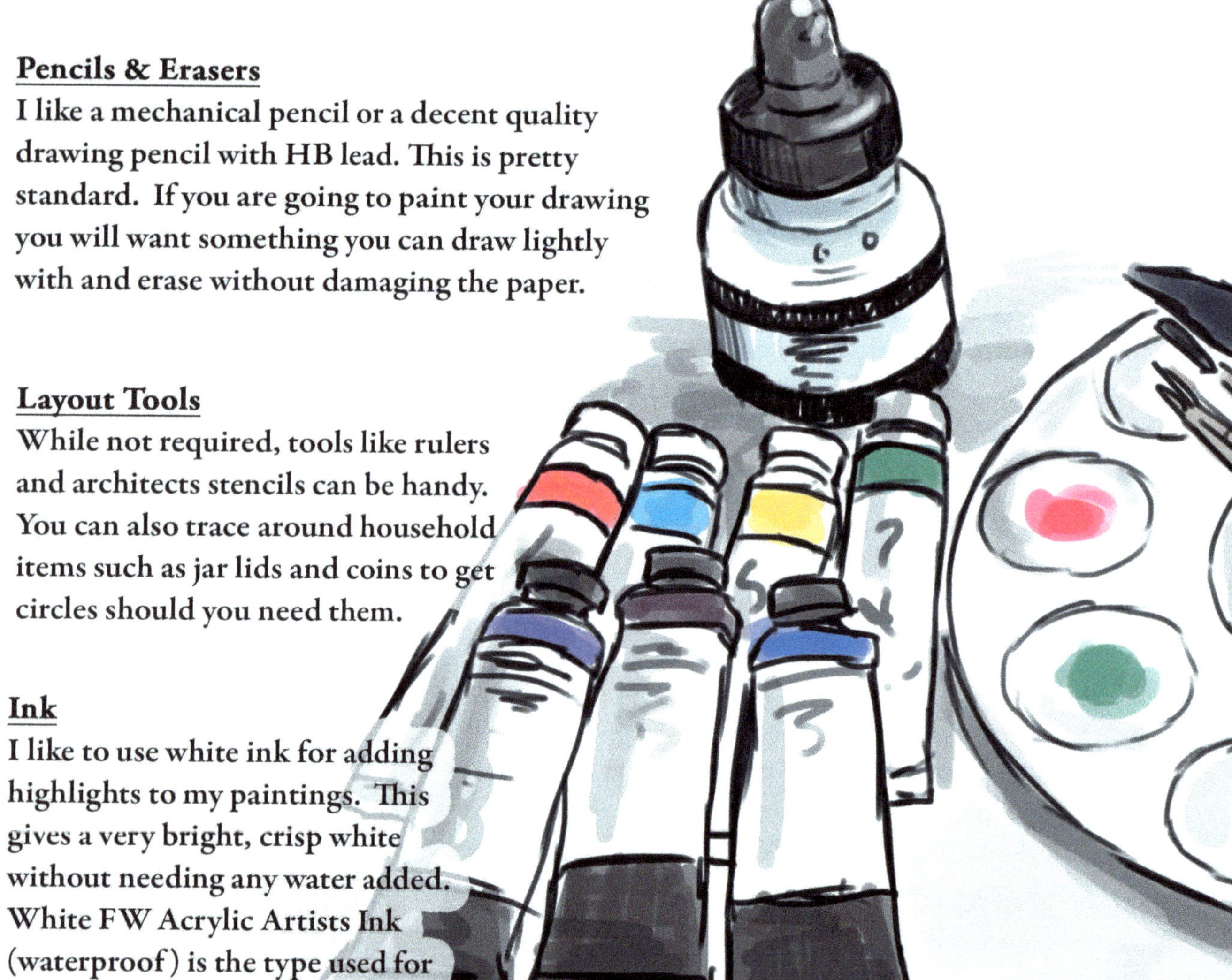

Pencils & Erasers
I like a mechanical pencil or a decent quality drawing pencil with HB lead. This is pretty standard. If you are going to paint your drawing you will want something you can draw lightly with and erase without damaging the paper.

Layout Tools
While not required, tools like rulers and architects stencils can be handy. You can also trace around household items such as jar lids and coins to get circles should you need them.

Ink
I like to use white ink for adding highlights to my paintings. This gives a very bright, crisp white without needing any water added. White FW Acrylic Artists Ink (waterproof) is the type used for the paintings in this book.

Watercolor

There are many brands of watercolor available. You can choose watercolors in a tube or paints that come in pans. I prefer to use tube watercolors and fill my own palette. If you plan to travel with your paints you should invest in a palette with a lid (but NOT airtight - you want your paints to dry when you are not using them).

You don't need many colors to start with. Lemon Yellow, Ultramarine Blue, and Permanent Rose are a good starting point. You can mix most other colors from these, but it is often handy to have a set with a variety of colors. A good quality student watercolor set should have everything you need and cost $8-$15 USD. If you want a slightly higher grade I recommend a set of Sakura Koi watercolors as they are still fairly affordable ($20-$35 USD) and have very vibrant colors.

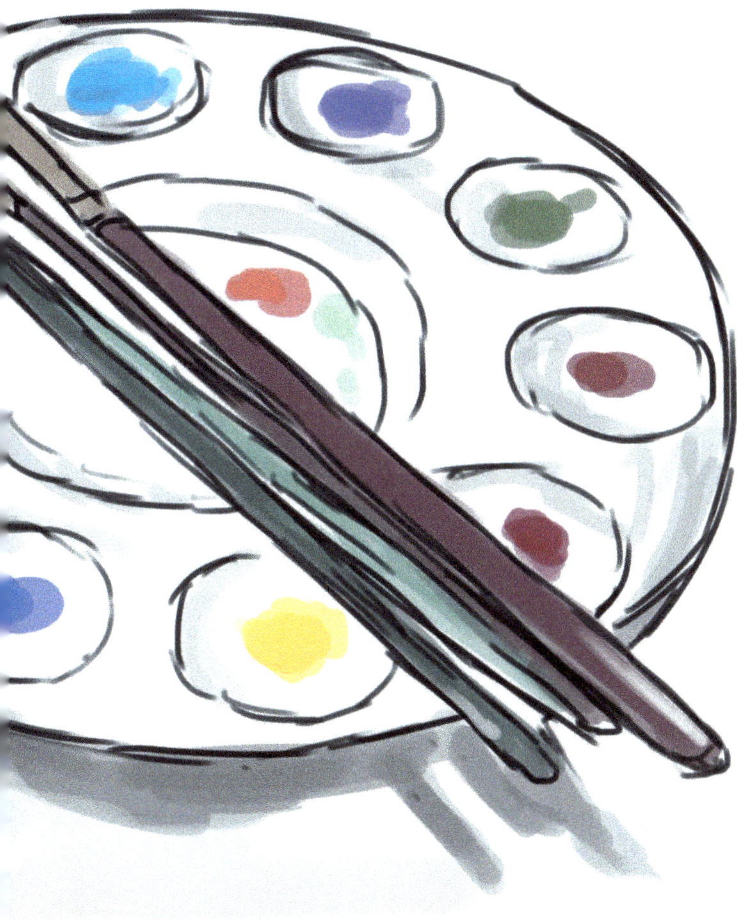

Brushes

I use Princeton watercolor brushes. These are affordable and come in many shapes and sizes. I suggest a larger "dagger" or "round" brush (4 or 5 in size) and some smaller round and/or "short liner" brushes for details (0 or smaller). The sizes you will need depend on the size you plan on painting. Experiment with sizes and shapes to see which brushes work best for you.

Paper

All the paintings in this book are on Canson XL Watercolor paper. It is durable, affordable, fairly easy to work with, and handles pencil, ink and watercolor well.

Features - Eyes

Here are some basic tips for drawing eyes. You can use these with any of the step by step dragon examples in this book to create your own unique dragon.

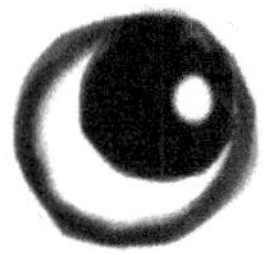 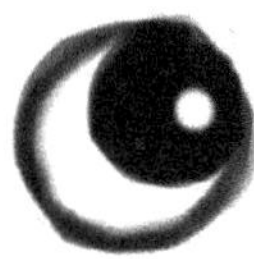 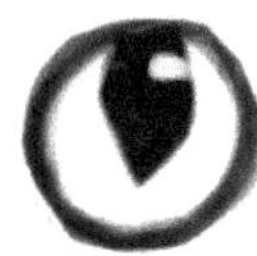 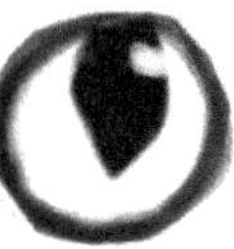 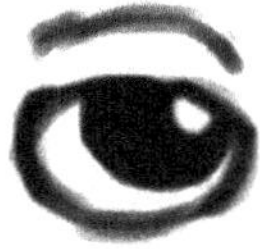 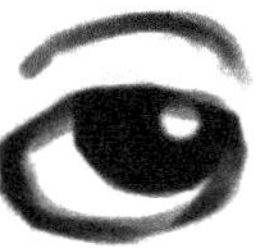

An eye starts with an eye ball - a circle. Inside this is a darker shape for the pupil of the eye. This could be round, or you can make more diamond-like shapes for a reptile look. If you show the entire circle of the eyeball with a large circle inside it this will create an innocent cartoon style baby dragon eye. If you want your dragon to look less wide eyed erase part of the circle and use the top of it to place the eyelids.

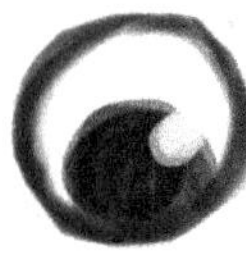 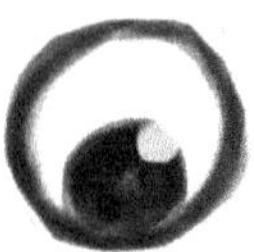 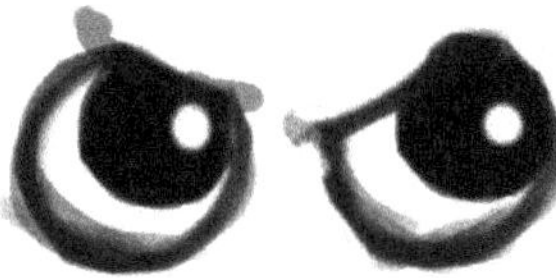 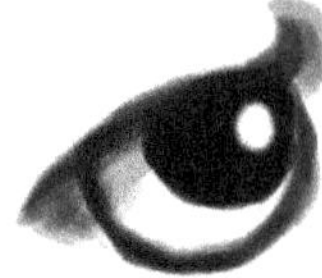 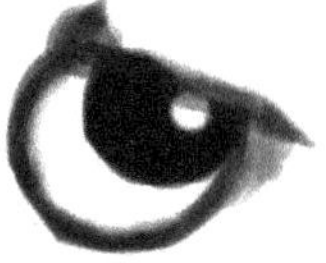

You can also move the pupils around in the eye to make the dragon look in different directions. Giving the eye an expression is easy - just change the shape of the eyebrows. You can also try moving the eyes closer together or farther apart.

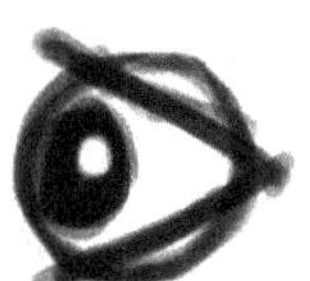

For a side view of an eye you still use a circle. The eye socket/eyelids form a sideways"V" shape around the circle.

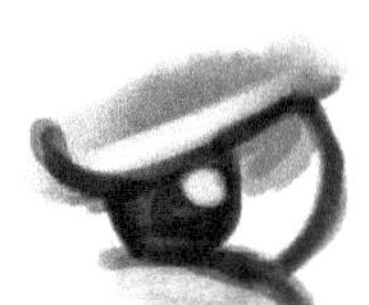 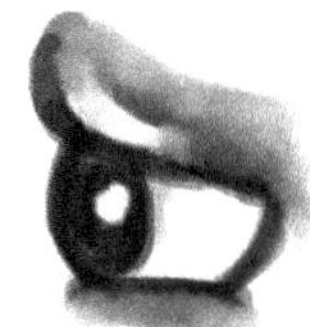

For more realistic eyes (less cartoon looking) make the pupil smaller and the eye less wide:

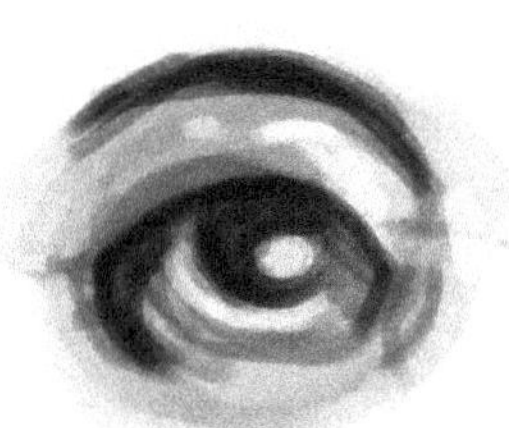 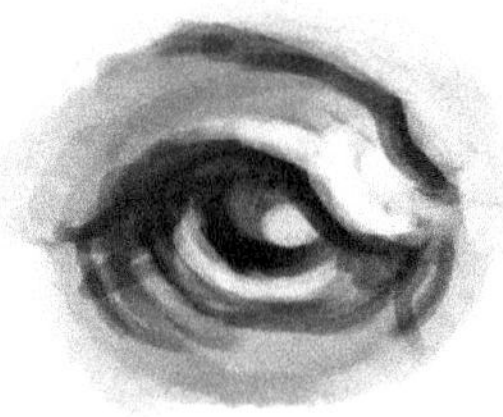 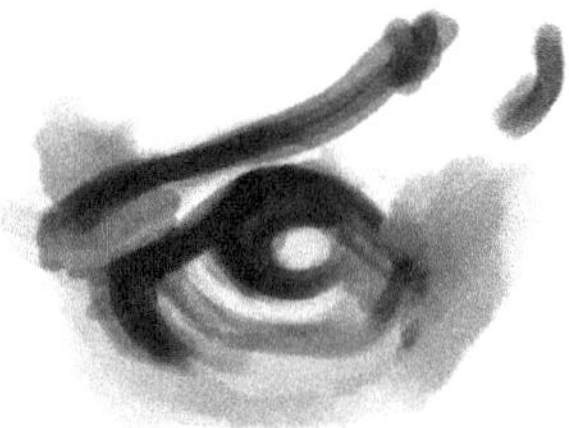

Features - Mouth & Nose

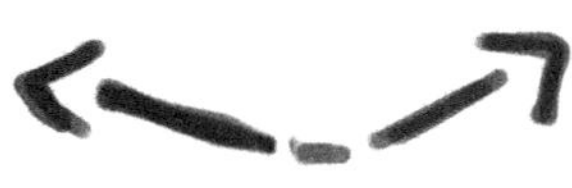

A mouth is easier to draw if you picture it as two arrows pointing away from each other. The points of the arrows suggest the cheeks. Then you can add teeth and suggest a chin.

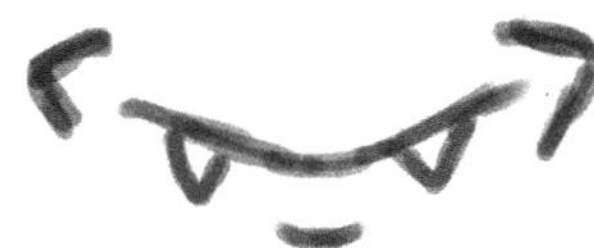

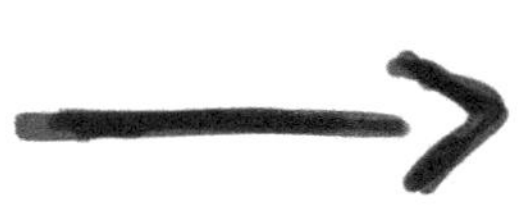

For a side view of the mouth use one arrow. For different expressions and to suggest teeth just make the line for the arrow wavy.

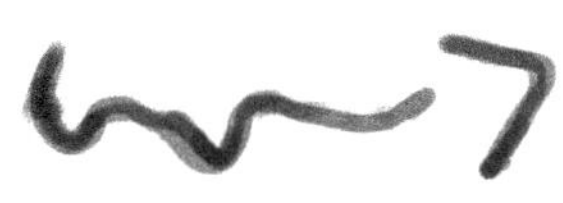

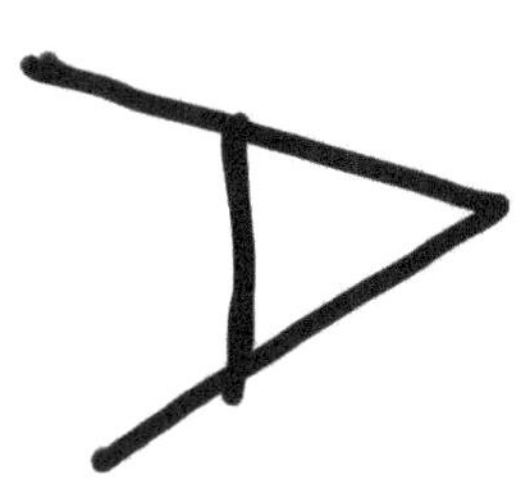

An easy way to draw an open mouth is to draw the letter "A" sideways. Then change the straight lines to add teeth and fill in the triangle part to show the inside of the mouth.

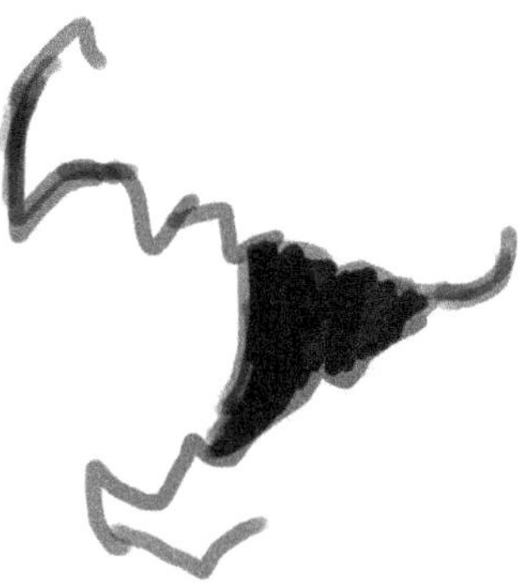

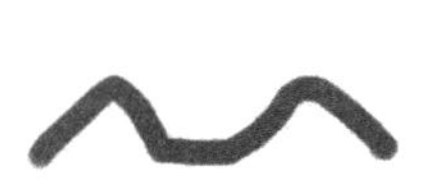

The nose can be drawn as a letter "M" shape that is a little more flattened out and wide. Then you can add two "C" shapes for the nostrils and a "V" shape for the tip of the nose.

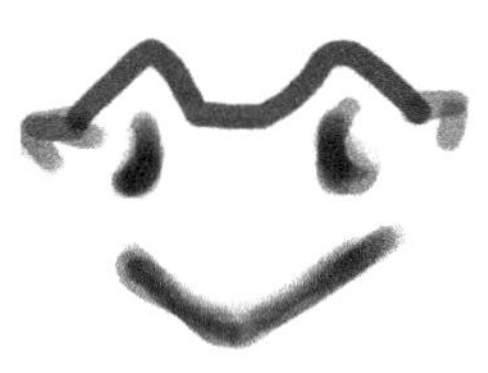

Side views of the nose can be a number of different hooked shapes. They might be more flat or curved, more dog like or more bird like. Try drawing a bunch of noses to see what works best for you.

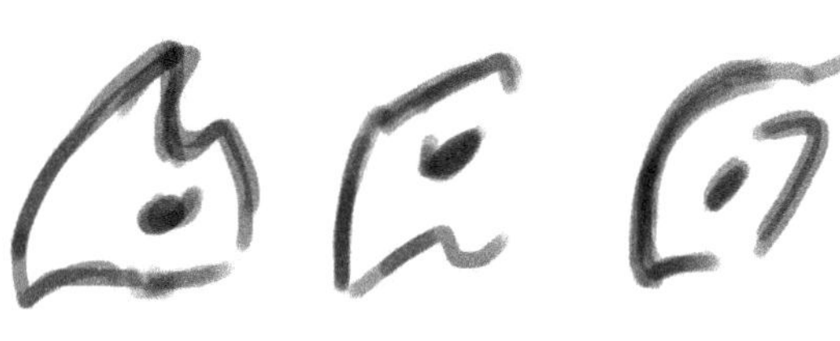

Basic Head - Wide

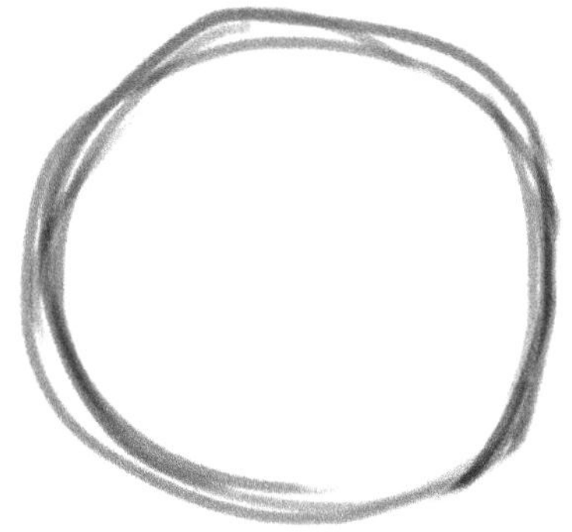

1. Sketch a circle

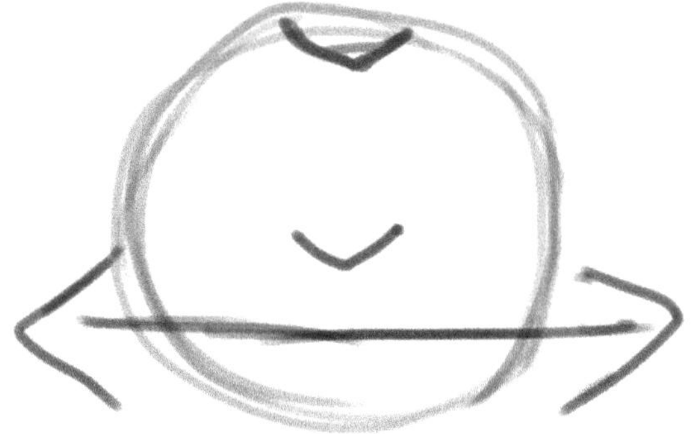

2. Add mouth line and four V shapes

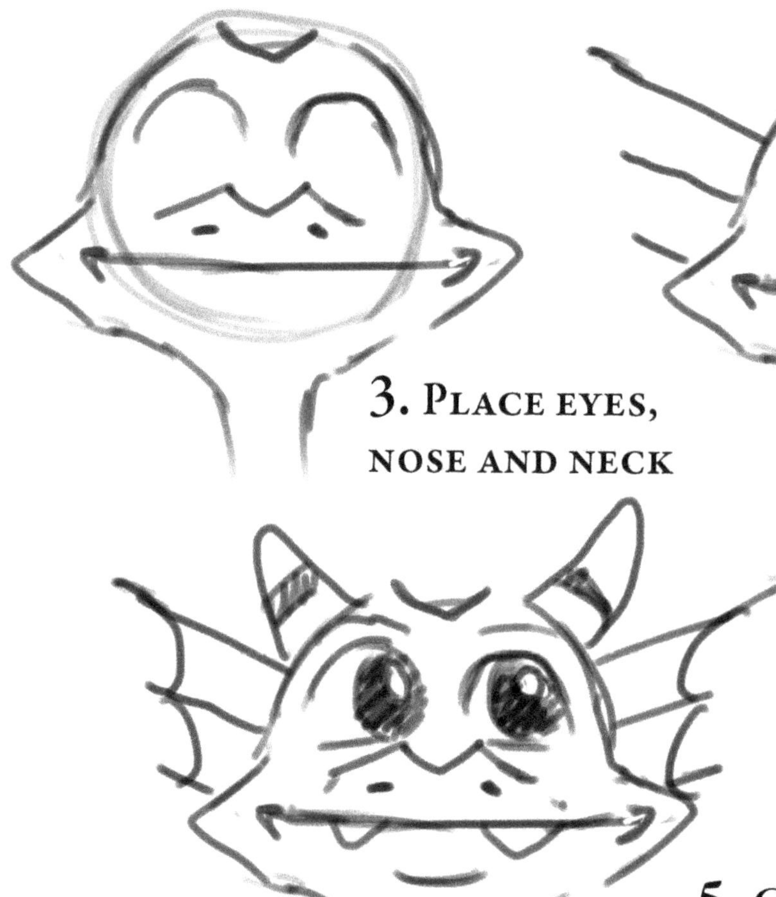

3. Place eyes, nose and neck

4. Add eyeballs and place ears

5. Clean up extra lines and add the details

Basic Head - Narrow

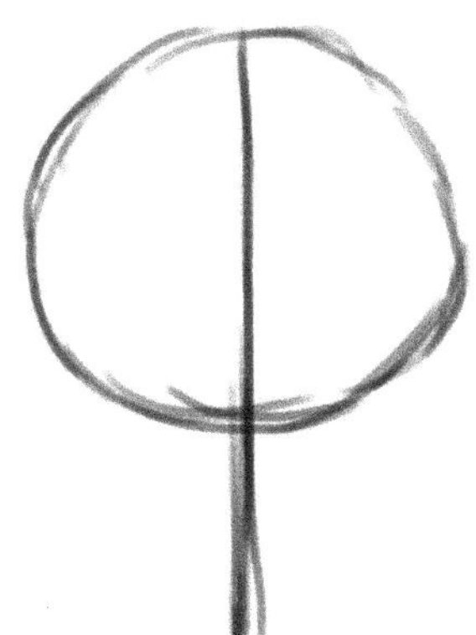

1. Draw a circle with center line

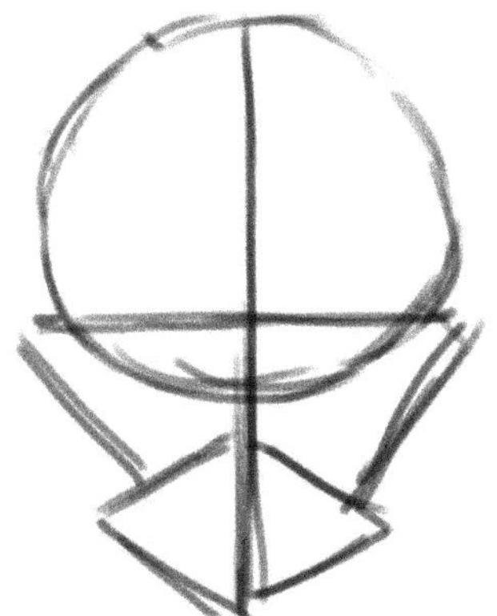

2. Draw two triangles for the nose and add the snout shape.

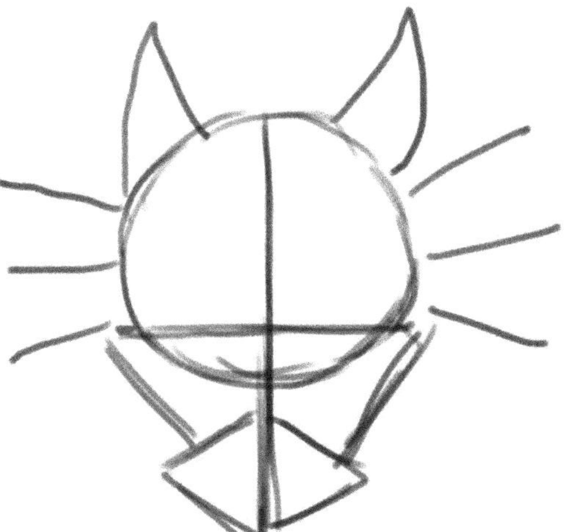

3. Place the horns and ears

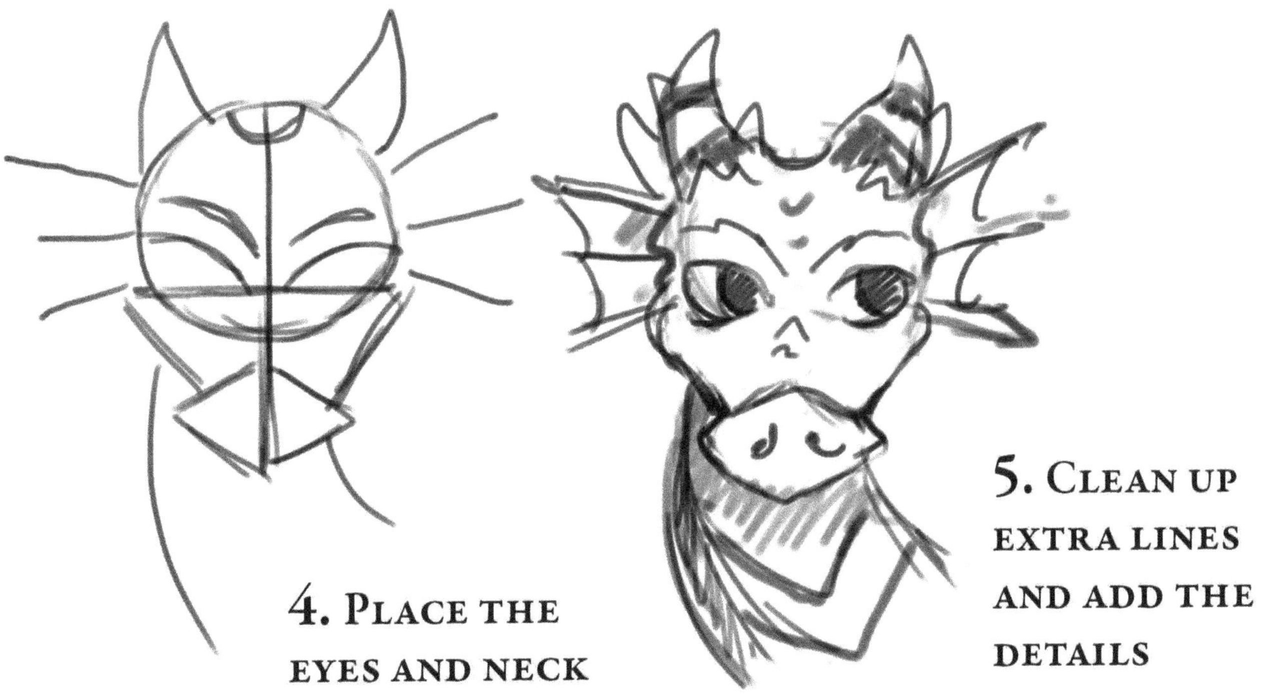

4. Place the eyes and neck

5. Clean up extra lines and add the details

Basic Head - Side

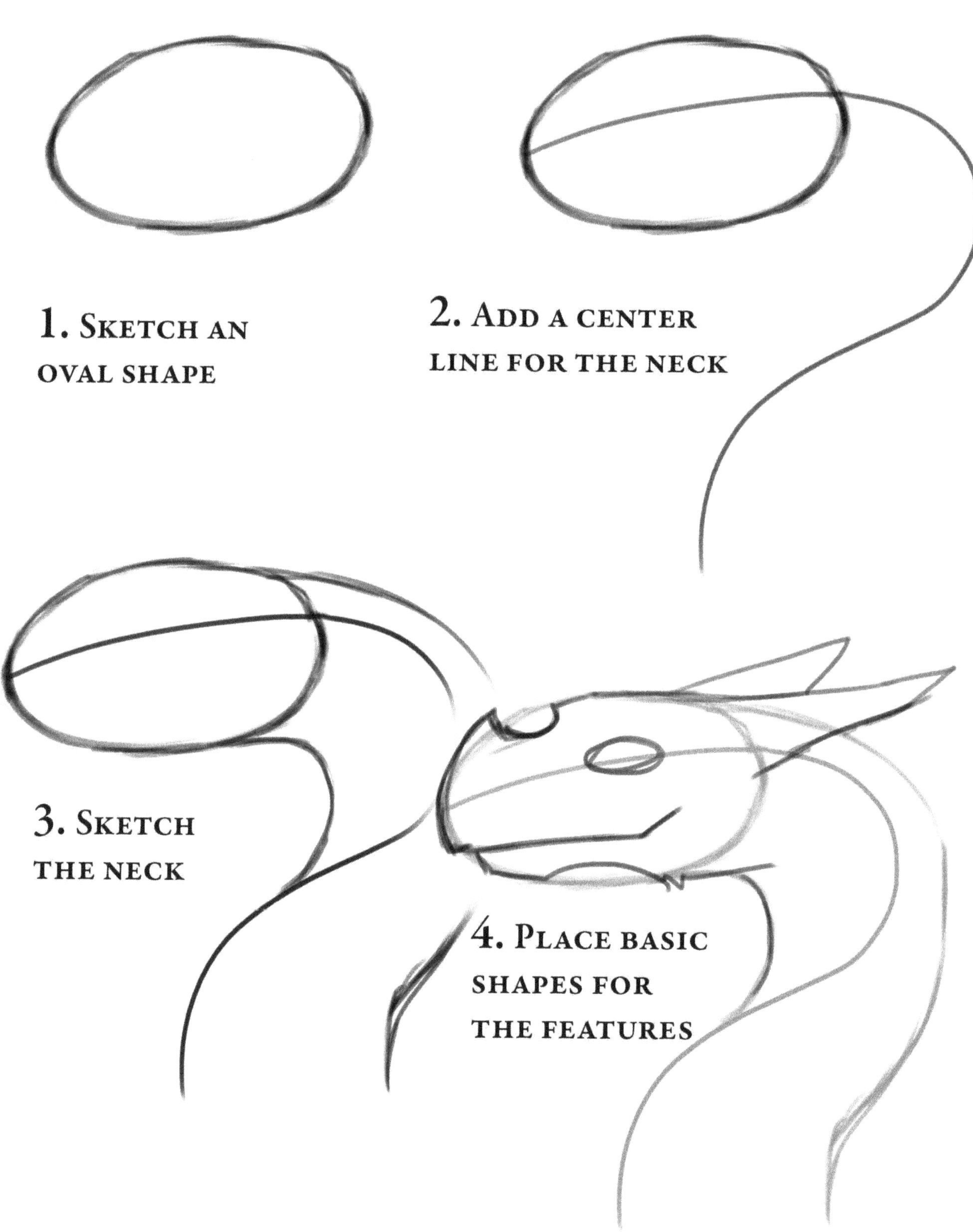

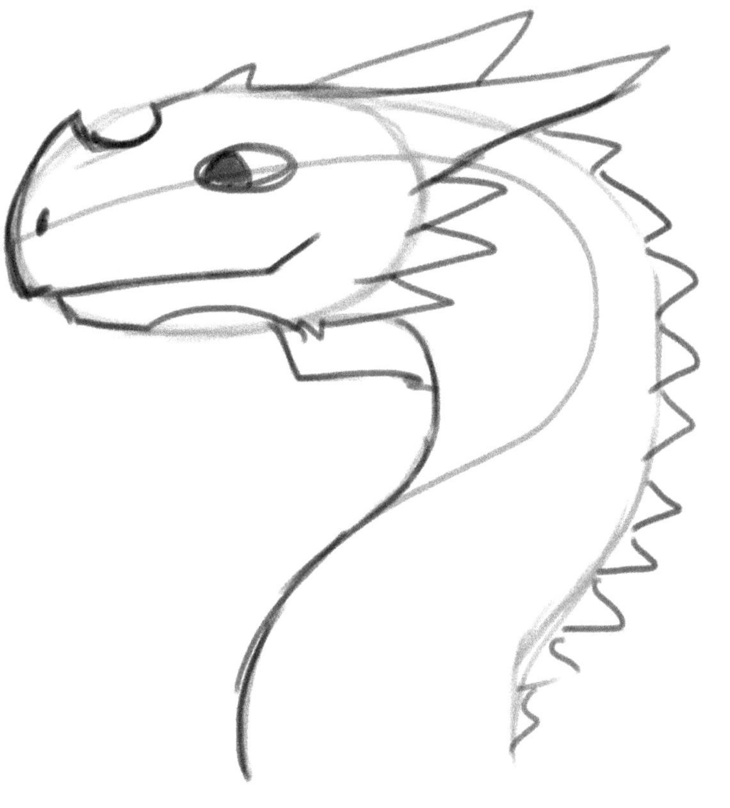

5. Refining the features

Now that you know where the features will be you can refine the shapes more to add the neck, back spikes, decide where the eye should look and so forth.

6. the details

Now clean up the extra lines and add the details for your dragon.

Watercolor 101

Watercolor is a water based paint. To make it darker or lighter you just add water. This is done by dipping your brush in water and using it to wet the paint. The more water the lighter the color, the more paint the darker the color. Watercolor is applied to paper in transparent layers called "washes." This means when you paint one color over another color, the color beneath will show through.

Using test sheets

Keep an extra piece of paper handy as a place to test your colors on first. This will let you see how they look blended together, layered over each other and so forth.

Work light to dark & large to small

Always start with the **lightest** colors and the **largest** areas. This will prevent you from washing away details when applying colors to the background and so forth.

Washes of the same color

Washing over the same color again will make it darker. This works well for adding shadows.

Combining different colors

You can layer one color over another to combine them. For example, if you paint blue on top of yellow you get green. You could also mix the blue and yellow before applying them to the paper which will result in a more uniform color.

Wet vs. dry

Watercolor applied to wet paper will blend into any color already there. If you want to blend colors together on the paper (such as for a sunset) it's a good idea to do this while wet. Watercolor applied to dry paper will not blend in, so wait for your paper to dry if you want to add details.

Practice makes perfect!

It takes time to get a feel for how much water and paint to use to get a given color. The more often you paint the easier this will get.

Using Basic Shapes

This book contains examples using basic shapes to plan a drawing and then adding details on top of them. You can use them to create the same dragons shown or as templates to create your own.

The dragons in this book are baby dragons. To make them look younger and cuter they have bigger eyes and more rounded lines. For adult dragons the lines are slimmer and more pointed, with longer horns and narrower eyes.

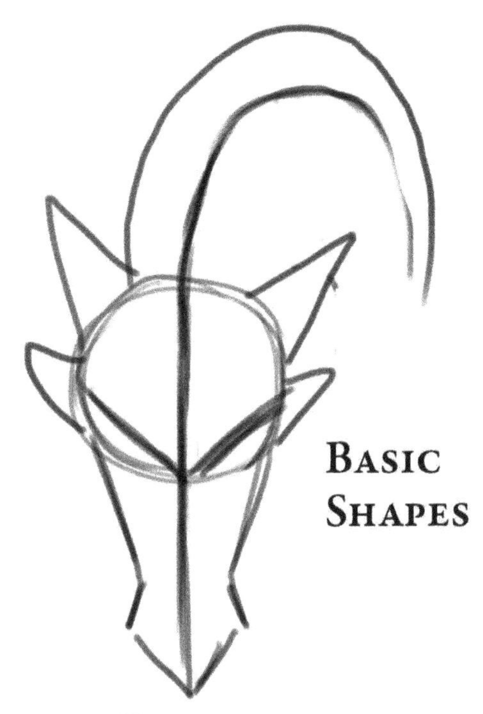

Basic Shapes

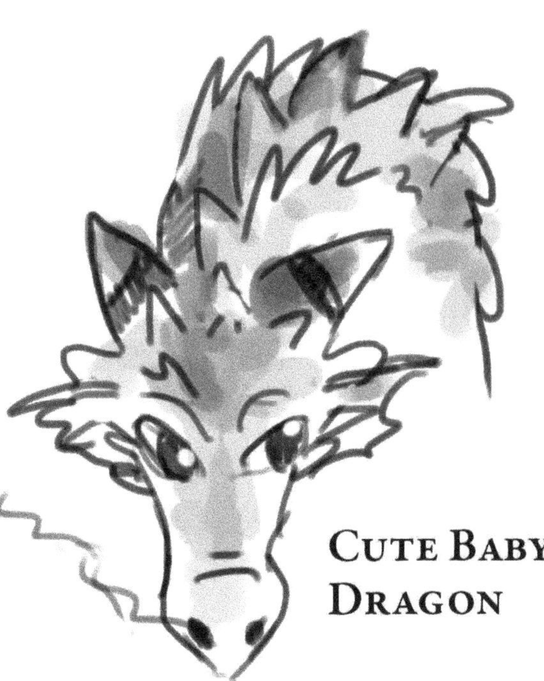

Cute Baby Dragon

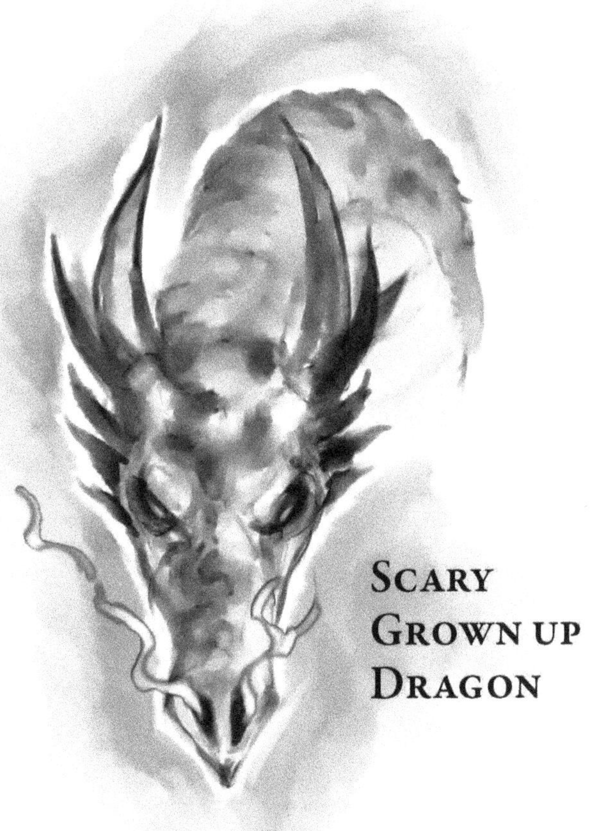

Scary Grown up Dragon

Teething Ice Dragon

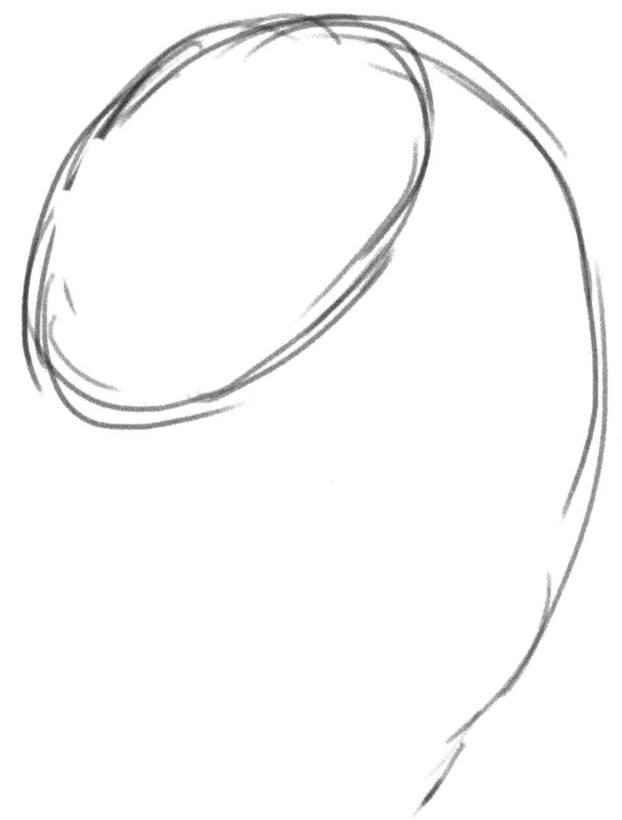

1. Sketch the head and neck

Start with an oval shape to place the head. Then draw the curve of the neck extending from it. Using these basic shapes you can place your dragon easily on the paper before adding the details.

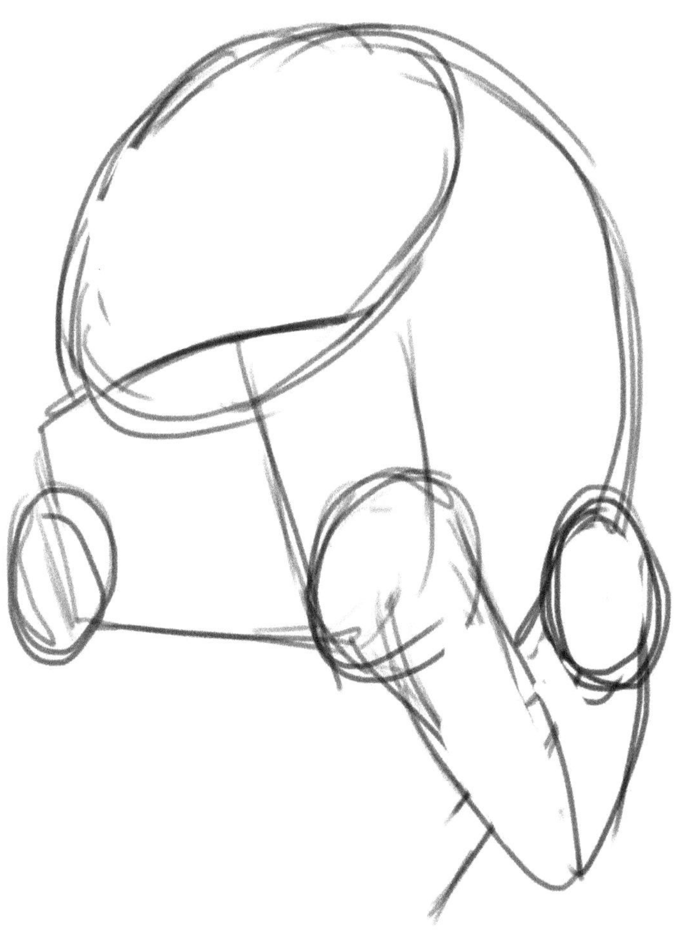

2. Place the limbs and ice cube

This baby ice dragon will be teething on an ice cube (of course!) so the next step is to sketch in where the arms and ice cube will be.

To place the arms use an oval or circle for the shoulder and another for the hands. Then connect them with lines for the arms.

3. Refining the features

Now refine the shape of the face to make the dragon biting the ice cube. This is easy to do by making a small "dent" into the side of the oval by the eye and then a line across for the nose.

Place the eyes and where the claws will be. Don't forget the teeth.

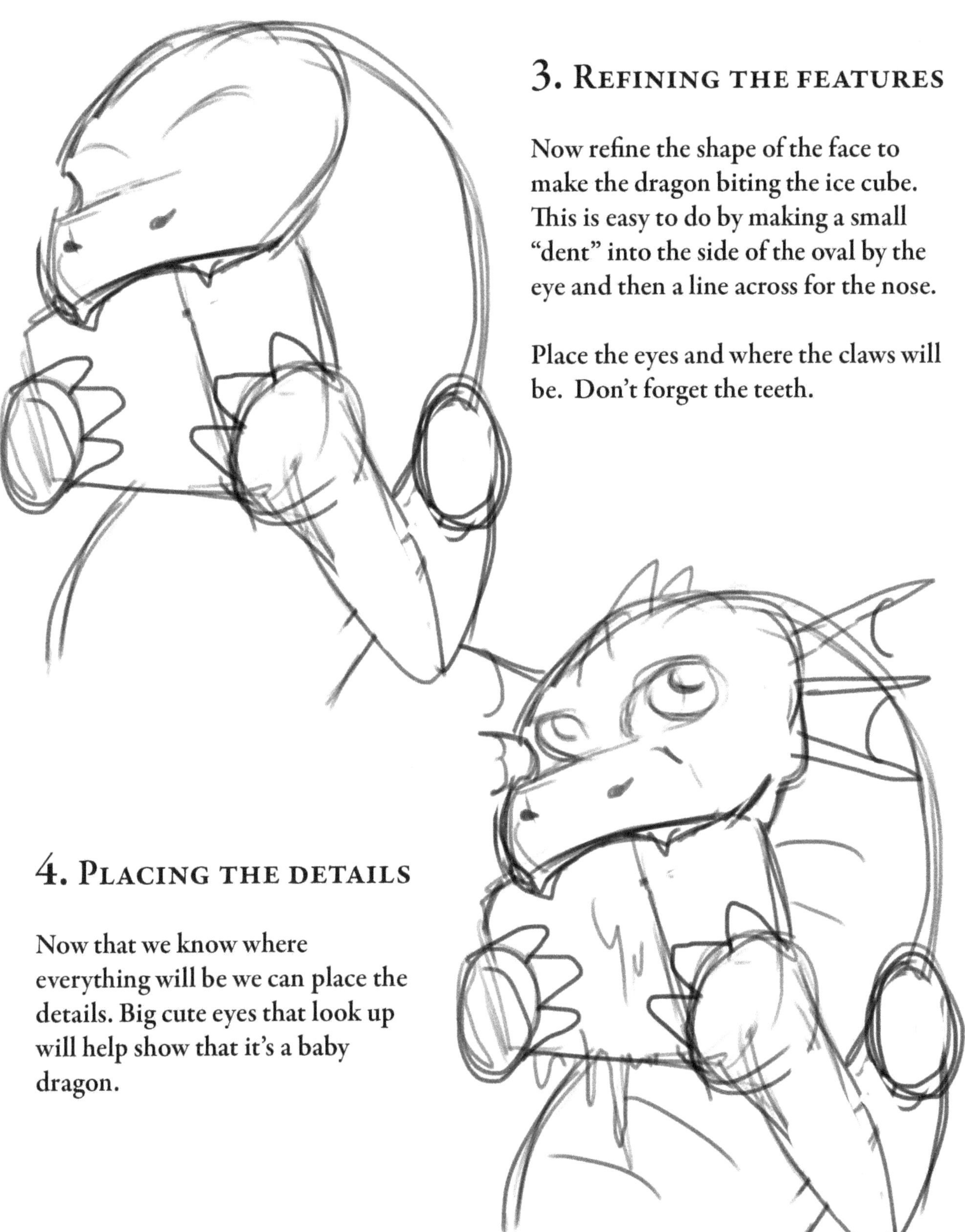

4. Placing the details

Now that we know where everything will be we can place the details. Big cute eyes that look up will help show that it's a baby dragon.

5. Clean Drawing

Use the basic shapes you planned out to create a clean and more detailed drawing.

This is accomplished by erasing the unnecessary lines and adding in details specific to an ice dragon such as icicles and blocky horns.

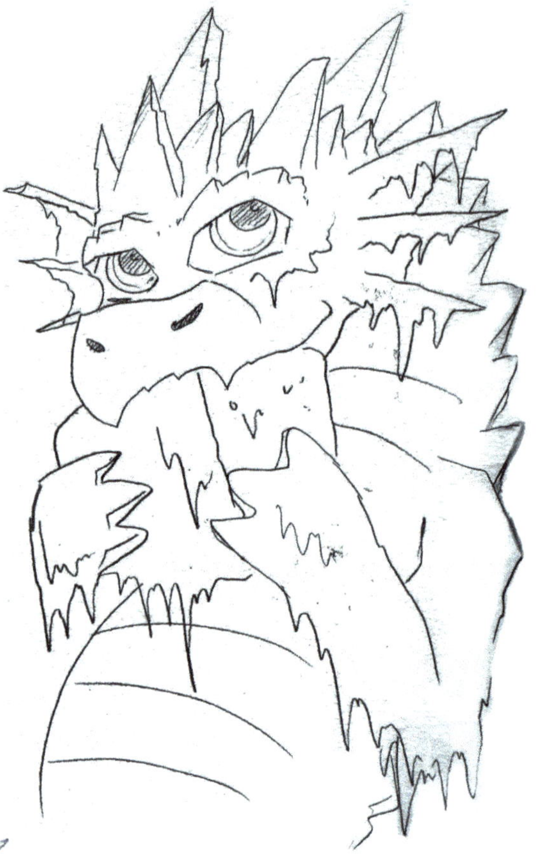

6. Under-painting

Paint the basic shadows using a teal blue.

Using more water results in lighter shades of blue, while less water creates darker shadows. Make sure to leave plenty of the white paper showing through.

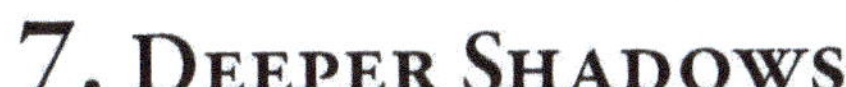

7. Deeper Shadows

Now use a medium blue (not as teal) to add darker shadows. You want to leave plenty of the lighter blue and white still showing.

Add a little violet (any purple shade you like will work) to the eyes and chest to give some color variation.

8. Details

Using a smaller brush add details with more blue. You can use a hint of a more purple blue like Ultramarine for the darkest areas (like the eyes) or mix purple with your teal blue.

Carefully paint over your original pencil lines with a small brush so they blend in with the rest of the painting.

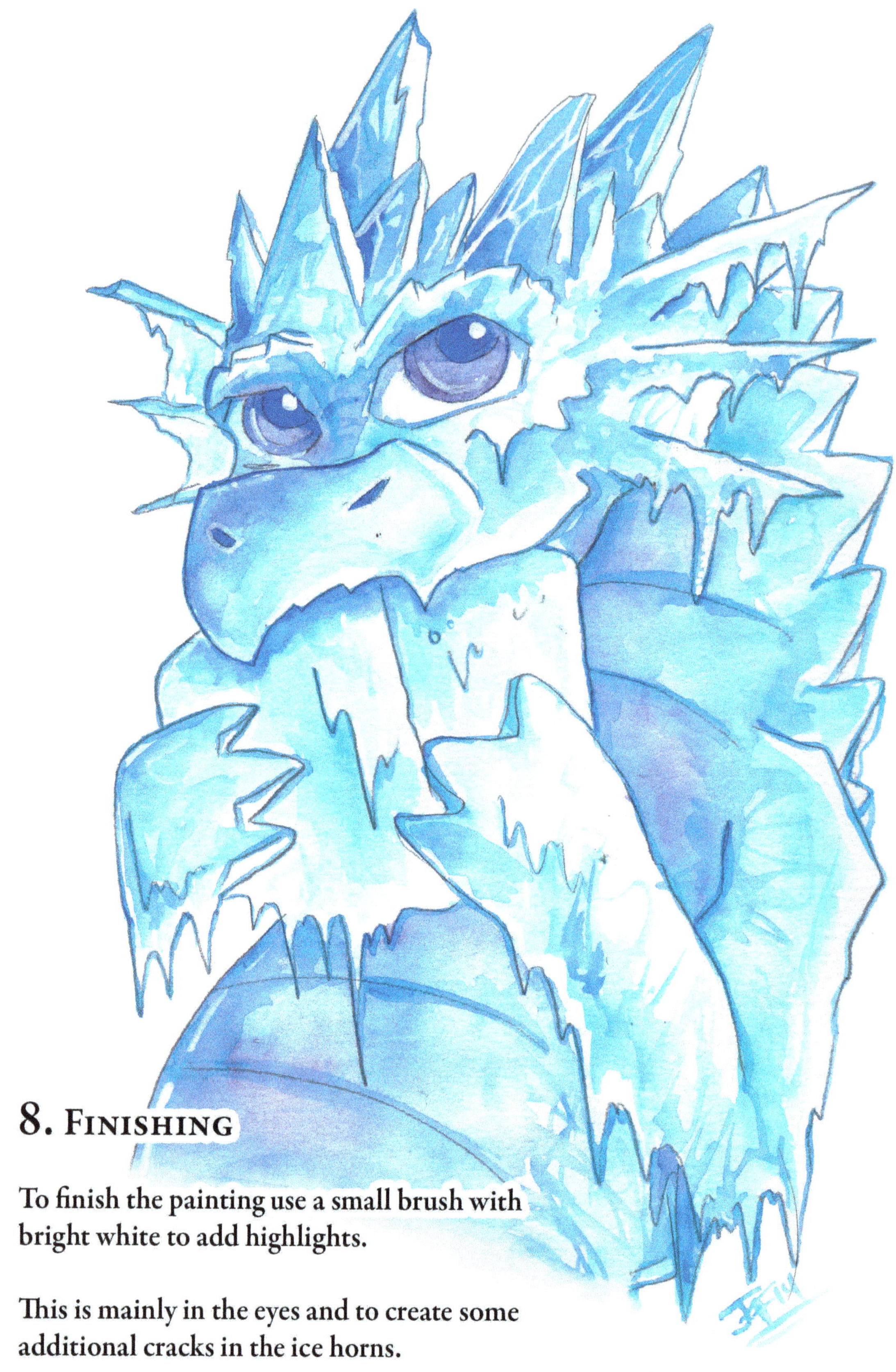

8. Finishing

To finish the painting use a small brush with bright white to add highlights.

This is mainly in the eyes and to create some additional cracks in the ice horns.

Painting Scales & Fur

Scales and fur are both textures you might find on a baby dragon. Here's some tips for drawing and painting them:

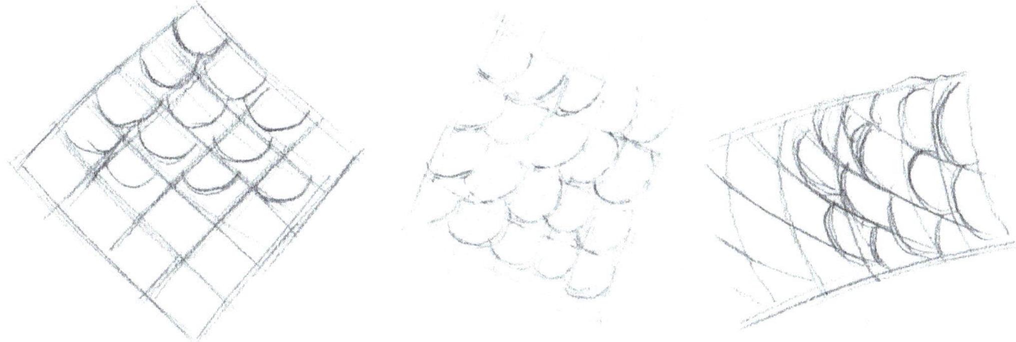

Scales

Use a grid to layout the scale pattern. This is basically small "C" shapes placed within each grid square.

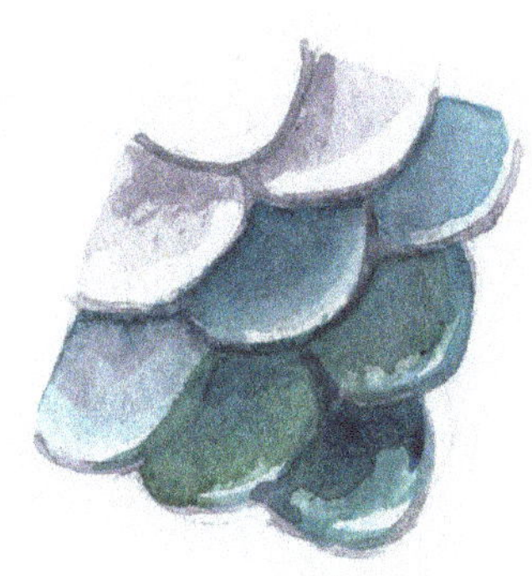

To paint the scales: first use a dark color to outline the scale and add the shadow. After this has dried add your first color. While that wash is still damp add a second color to create variation. Allow to dry and then darken shadows as needed.

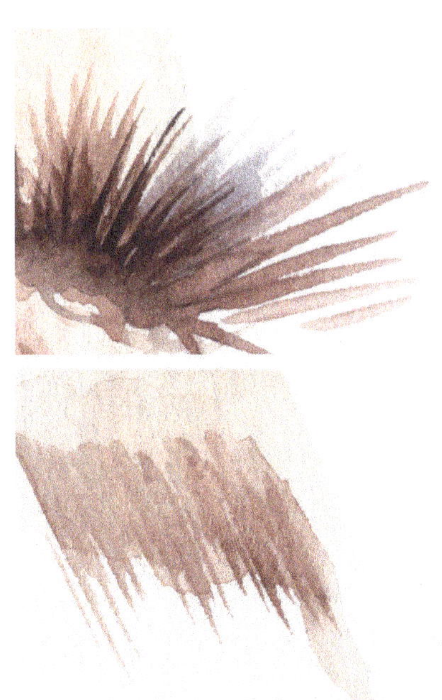

Fur

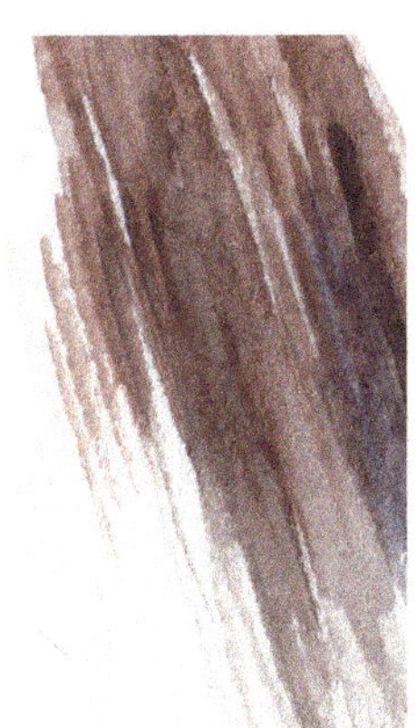

There are a number of textures for fur depending on if it is sticking up or flat and hair like. These different looks can be achieved by trying out different brush strokes with round and square ended brushes.

Start with a light base color and let it dry. Then use a smaller brush to "pull" lines in the shape of the fur. Start with a medium color, let dry, and repeat with an even darker color to create layers of fur.

Furry Snow Dragon

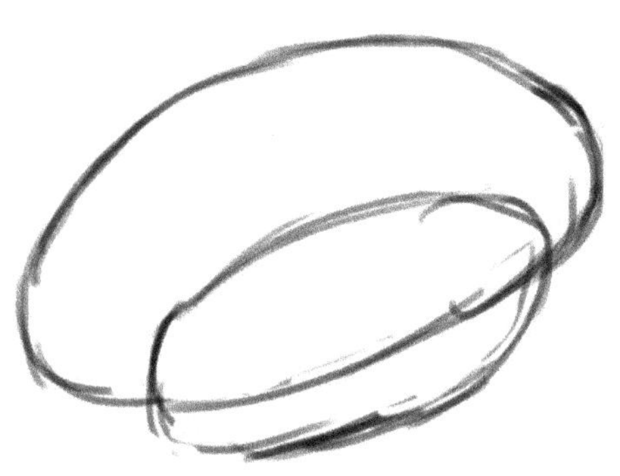

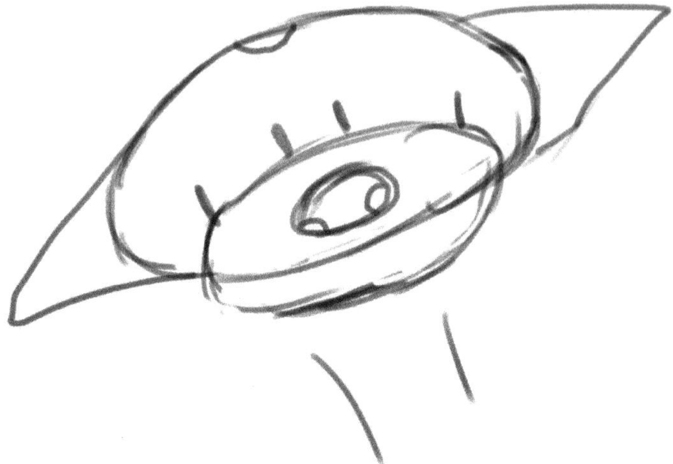

1. Head and Snout

Start with two overlapping oval shapes. The larger one is for the head and the smaller one is for the snout.

2. Place the features

Next draw in two triangles for the ears and two lines for the chest. Make a small "V" shape in the top of the head. Plan where the eyes will go with two lines and add a circle for the nose.

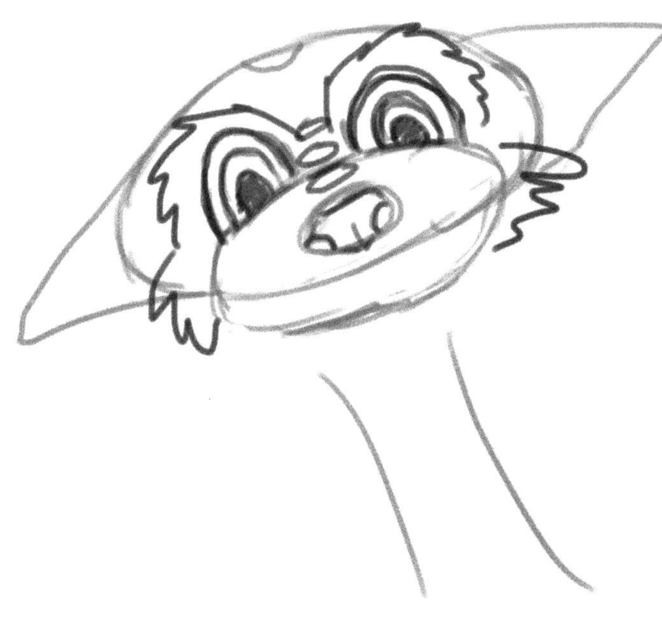

3. Face and fur!

Now you can use your guidelines to draw in some fun fluffy fur and add the eyes. Drawing fur is easy - it's just a zaggy scribble like this:

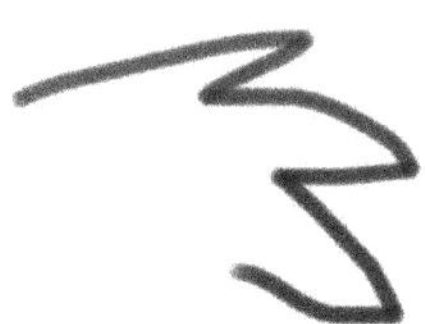

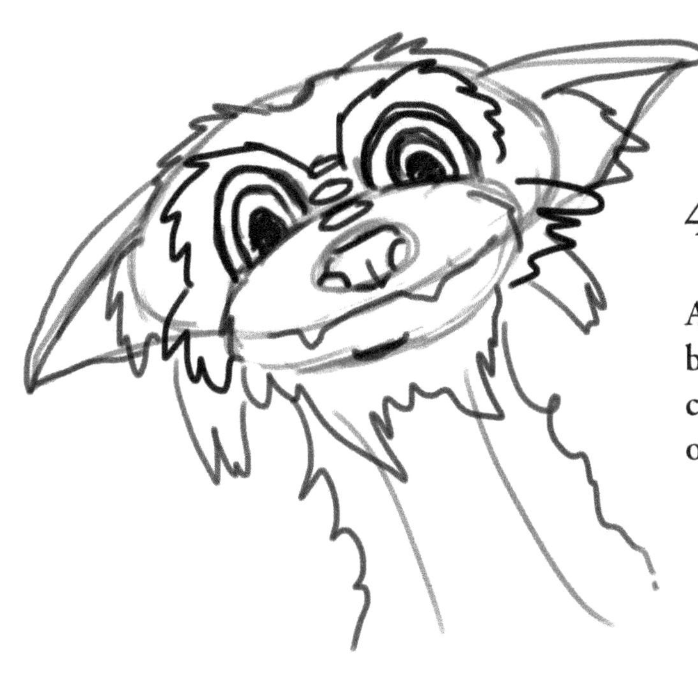

4. Adding the details

Add more fur and the shape of the body. Add teeth and a suggestion of a chin. Don't forget some fur hanging off the chin and out of the ears!

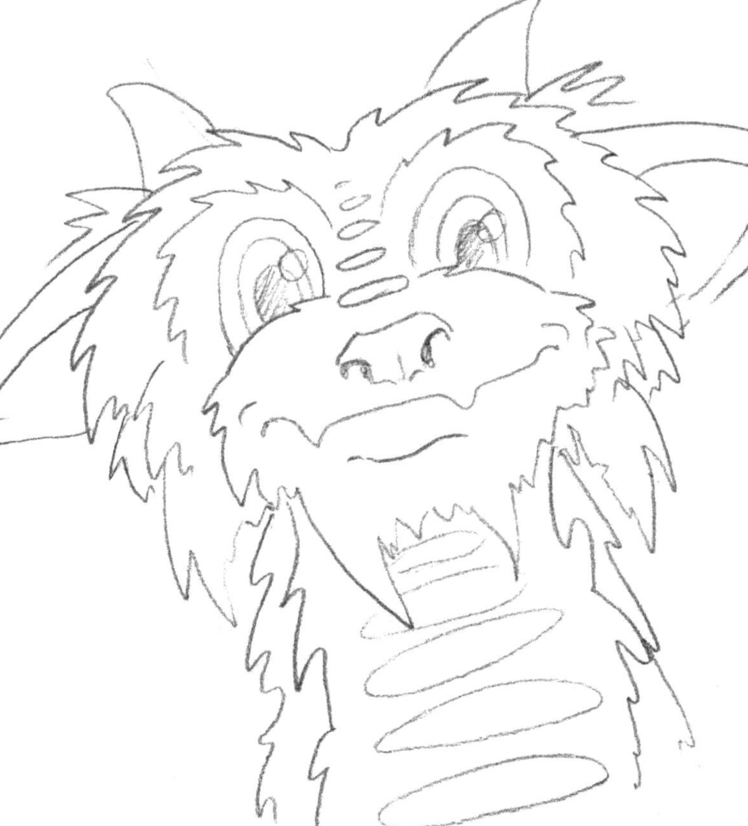

5. Clean Drawing

Use the basic sketch you did to create a more detailed and cleaner drawing that is ready for paint. You can give him, horns, a pattern on his neck, lots of fur and any other details you like.

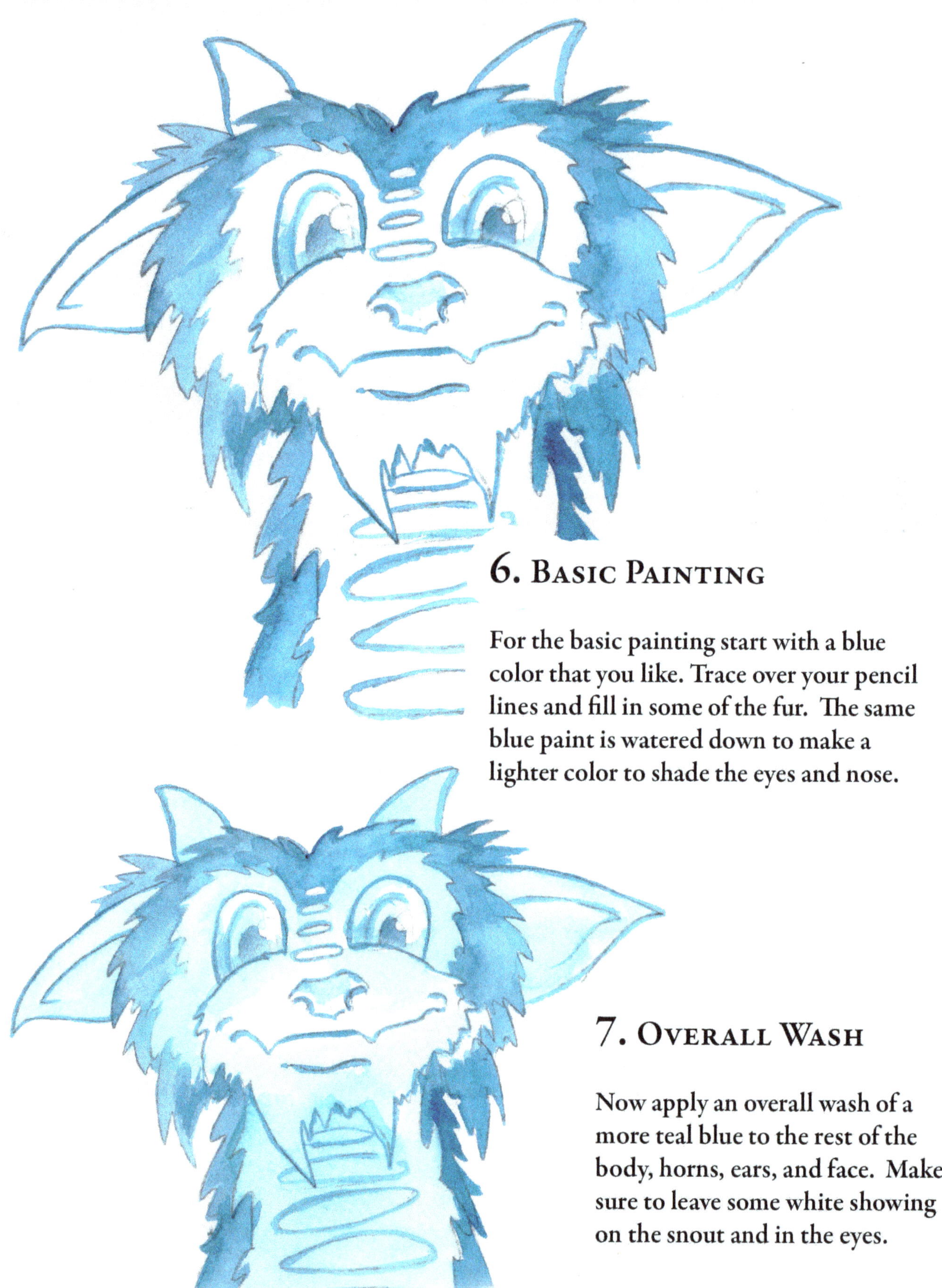

6. Basic Painting

For the basic painting start with a blue color that you like. Trace over your pencil lines and fill in some of the fur. The same blue paint is watered down to make a lighter color to shade the eyes and nose.

7. Overall Wash

Now apply an overall wash of a more teal blue to the rest of the body, horns, ears, and face. Make sure to leave some white showing on the snout and in the eyes.

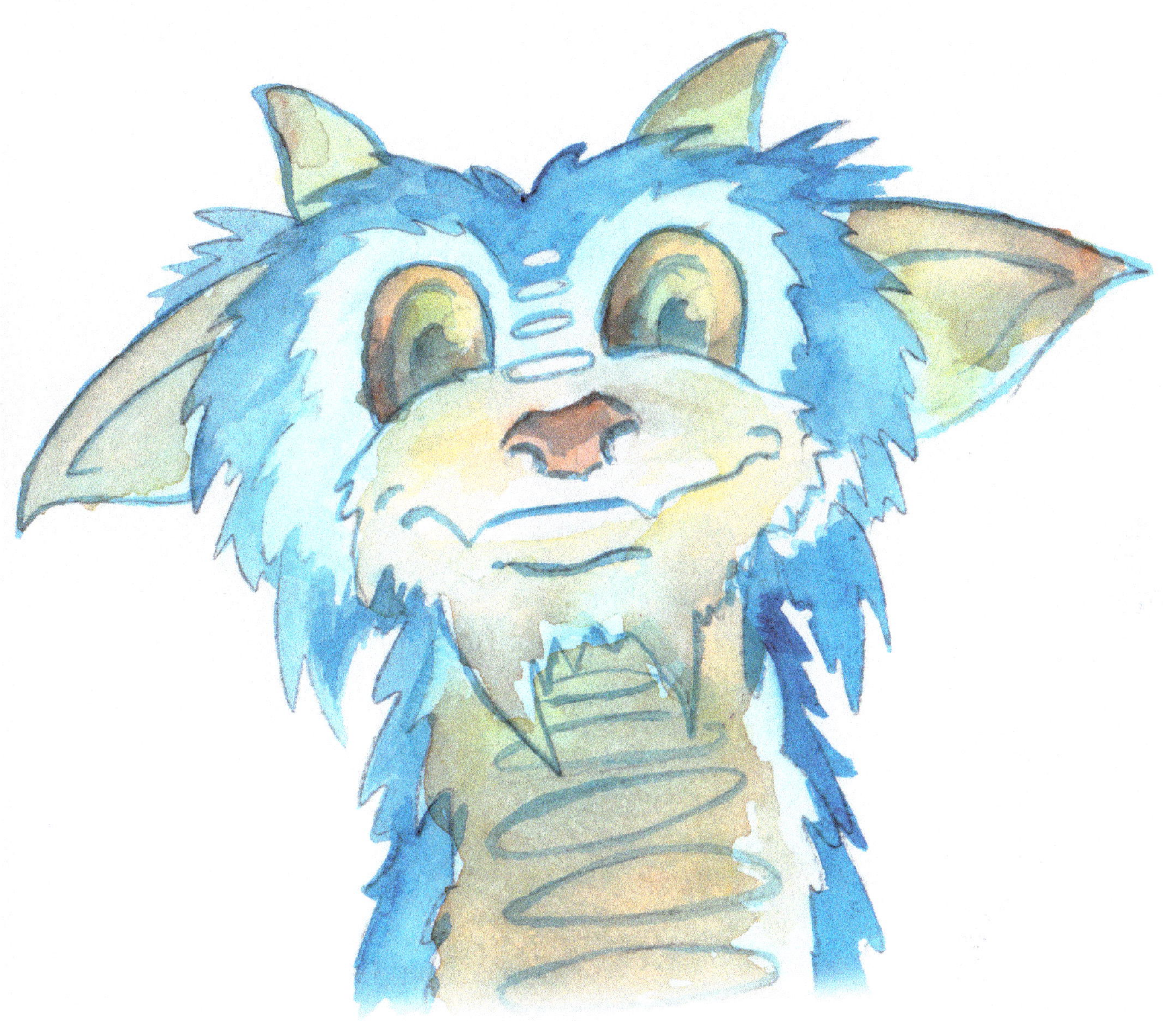

8. Color Variation

The next part is really fun! You need two colors for it: a orange-yellow and an orange-red.

First apply a light wash of the orange-yellow color to the horns, ears, eyes, snout and chest. Note that we are leaving the darker blue fur and fur around the eyes as it is.

Then apply the more red-orange very watered down to the nose, tips of the ears, and lower/outer part of the eyes.

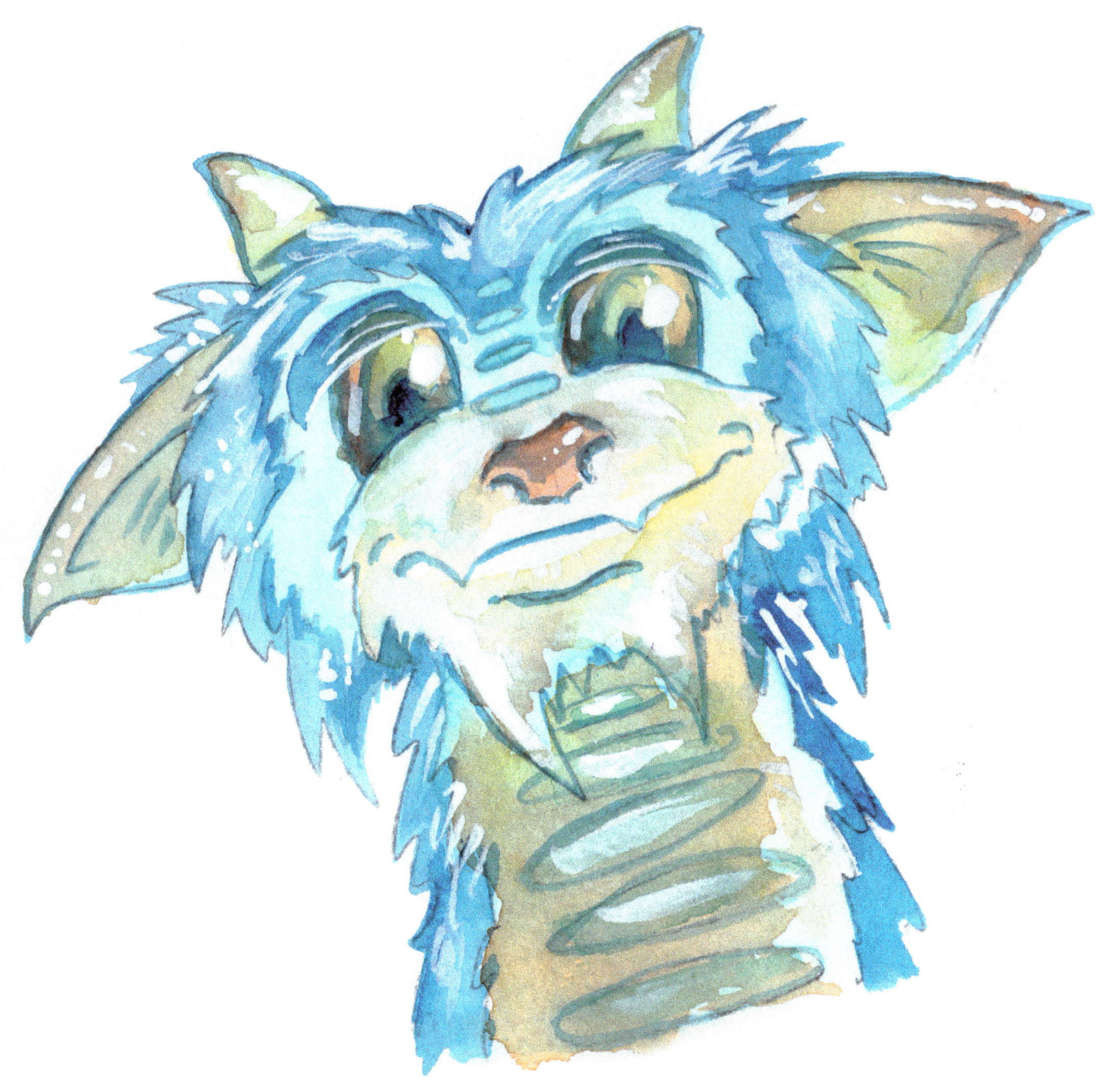

8. Finishing Touches

Time to finish up our Snow Dragon! Now go back to your original blue color and use it to darken the eyes and paint eyelids over the top for a more sleepy look. Once this has fully dried use bright white paint or ink to add highlights. These are added in the eyes, on the horns and chest, and to make the fur have depth.

Holding a Leash

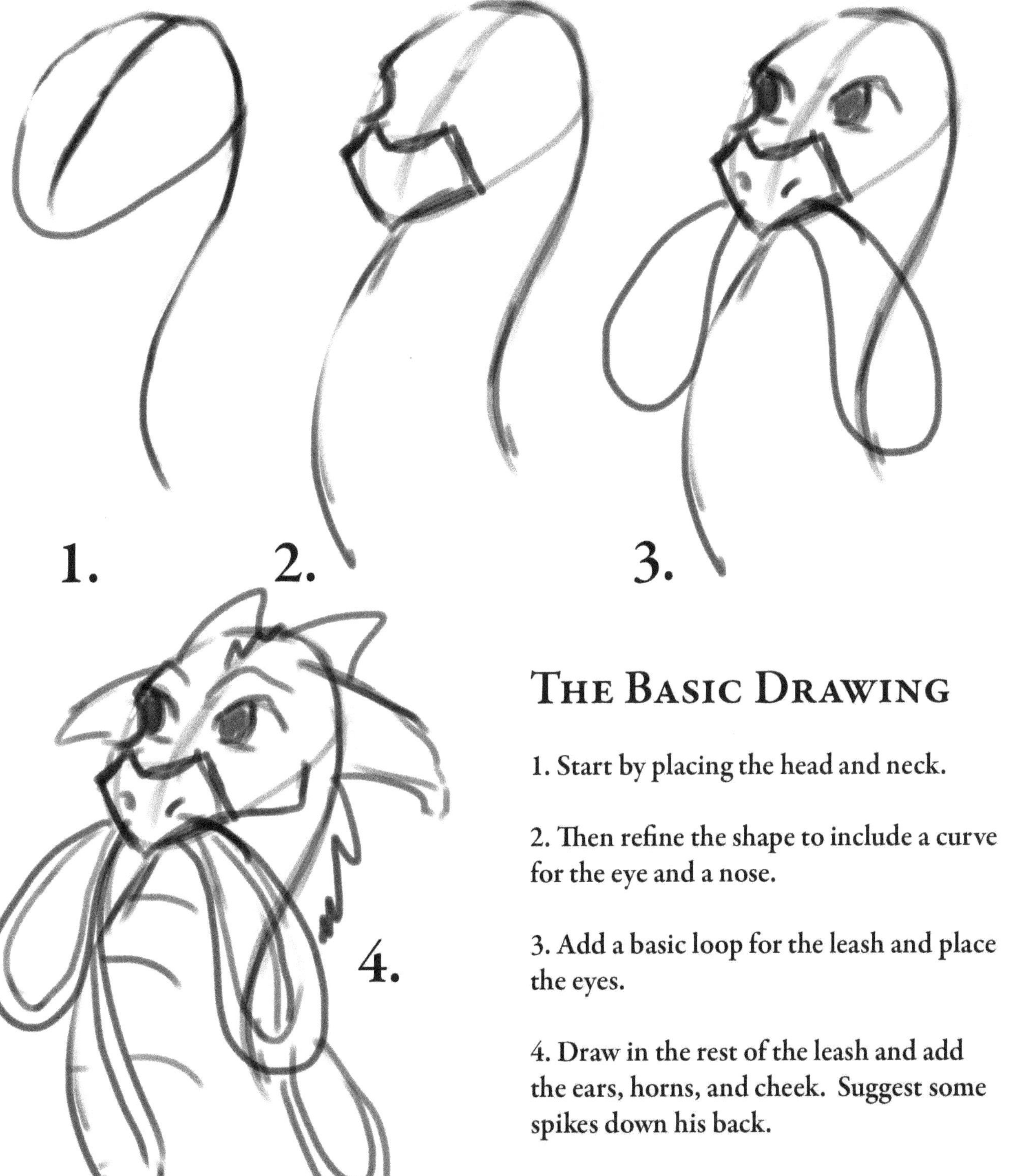

The Basic Drawing

1. Start by placing the head and neck.

2. Then refine the shape to include a curve for the eye and a nose.

3. Add a basic loop for the leash and place the eyes.

4. Draw in the rest of the leash and add the ears, horns, and cheek. Suggest some spikes down his back.

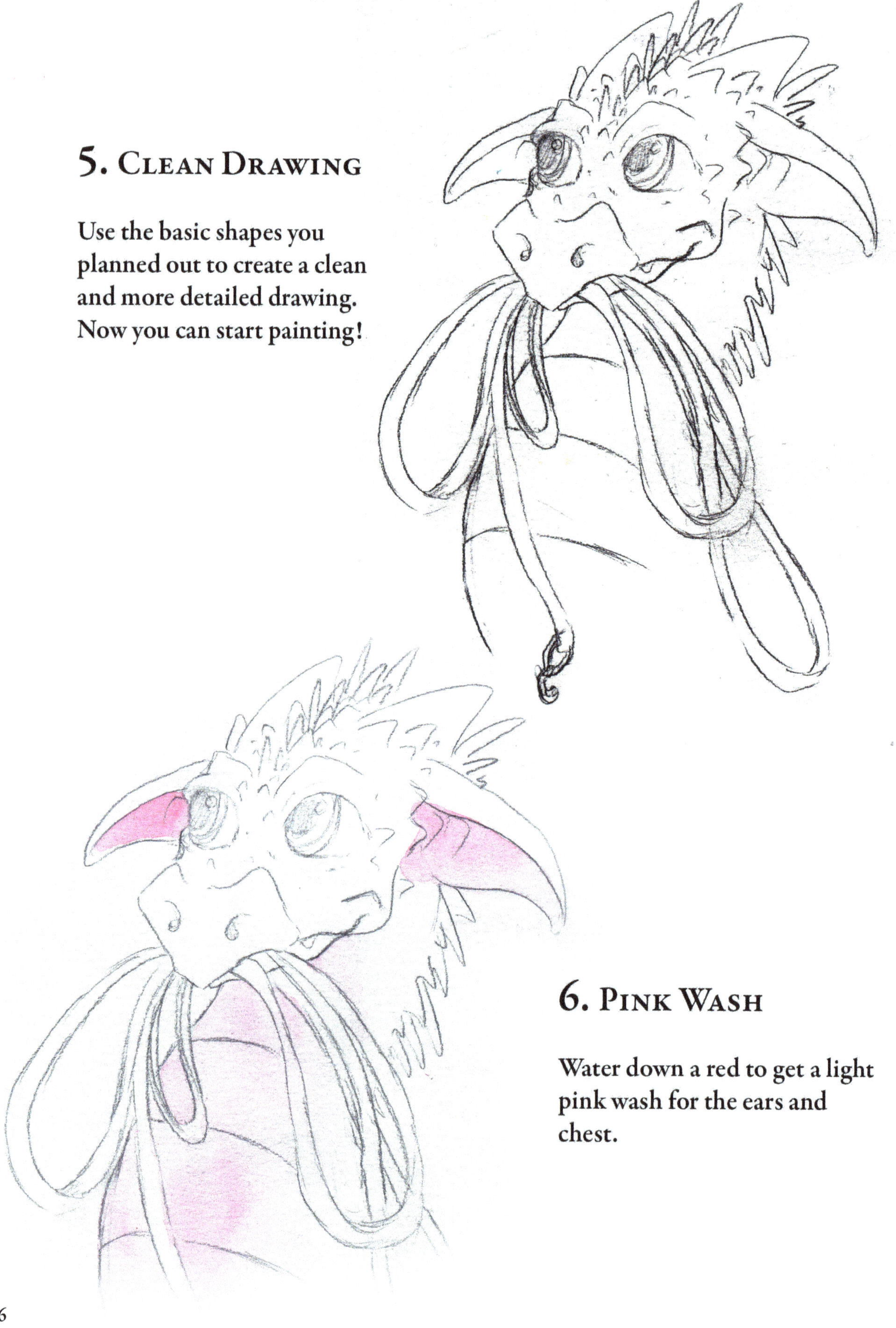

5. Clean Drawing

Use the basic shapes you planned out to create a clean and more detailed drawing. Now you can start painting!

6. Pink Wash

Water down a red to get a light pink wash for the ears and chest.

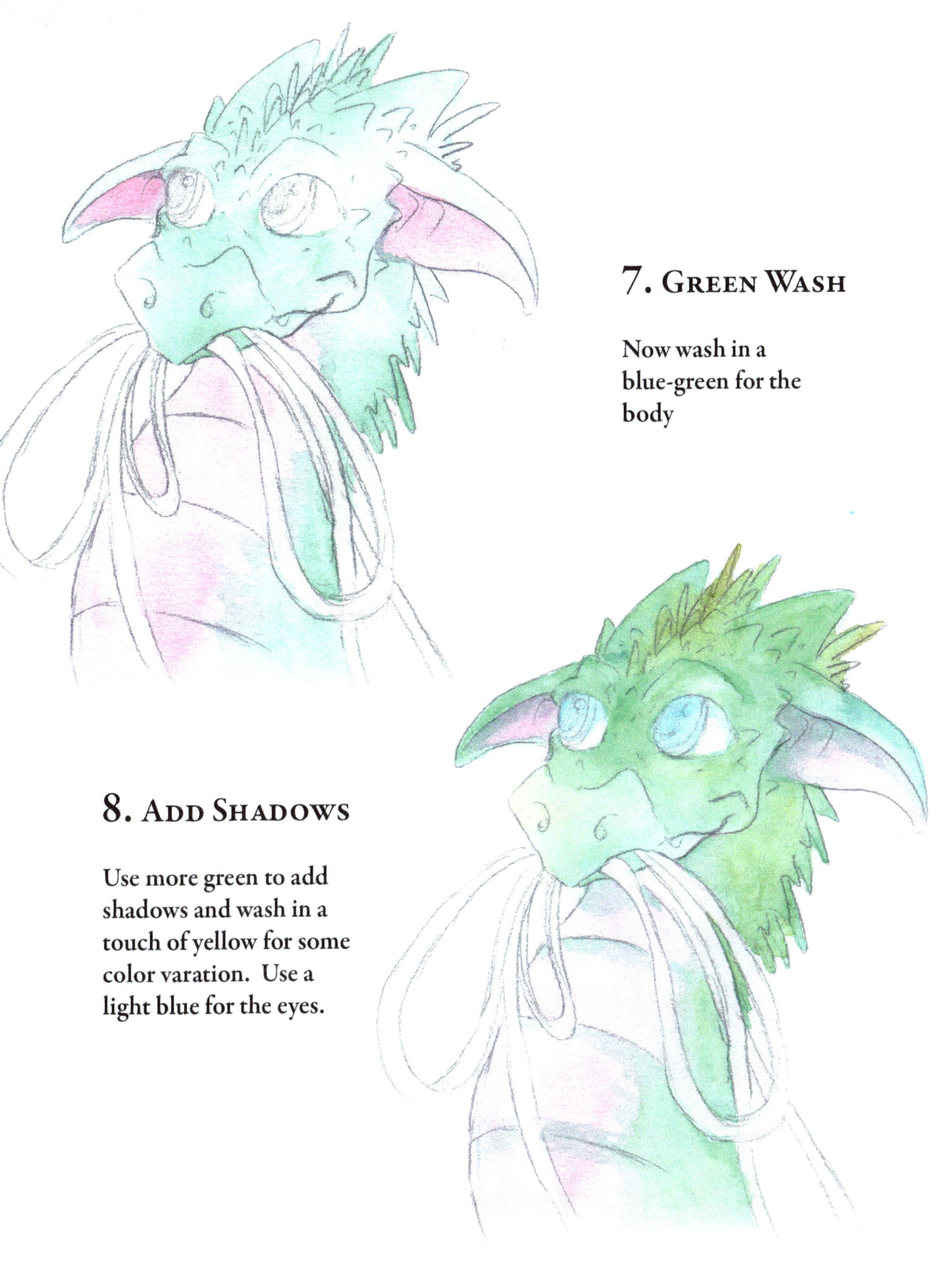

7. Green Wash

Now wash in a blue-green for the body

8. Add Shadows

Use more green to add shadows and wash in a touch of yellow for some color varation. Use a light blue for the eyes.

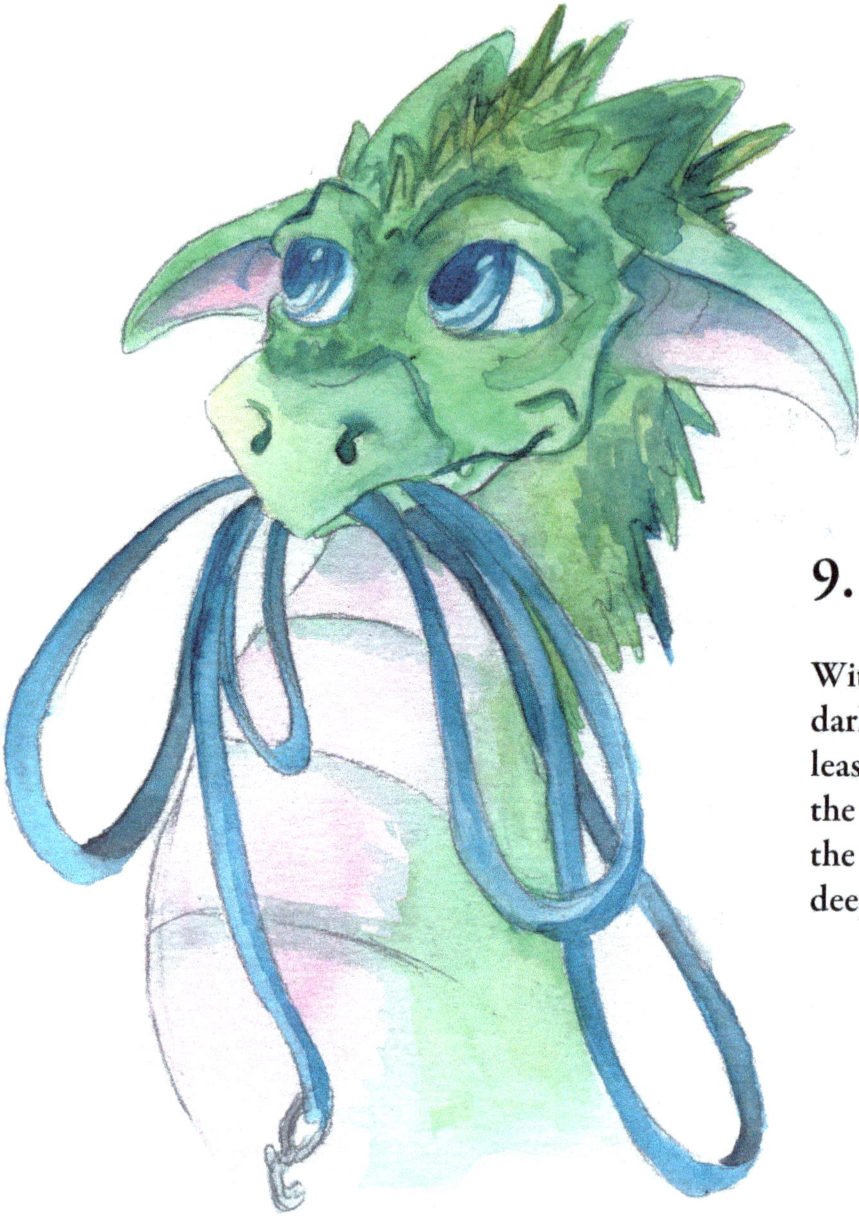

9. Add Details

With a small brush use a darker blue to finish the leash and add details to the eyes as well as making the shadows and lines deeper.

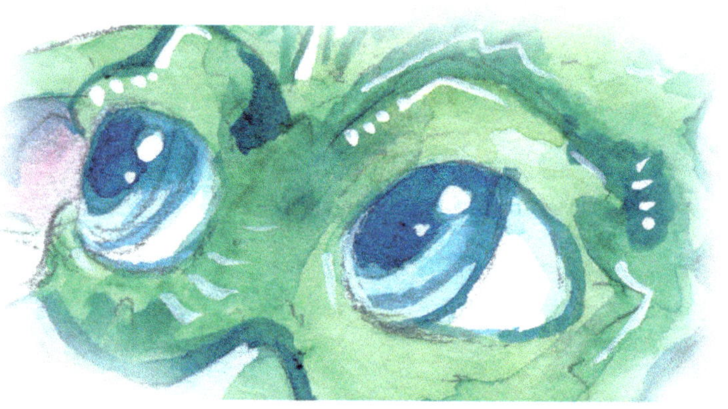

10. Finishing up

Using your smallest brush and some bright white paint (or ink) add in the highlights. These appear on the eyes, nose and anywhere needed to make the painting "pop".

CAN WE GO FOR A WALK **NOW**?

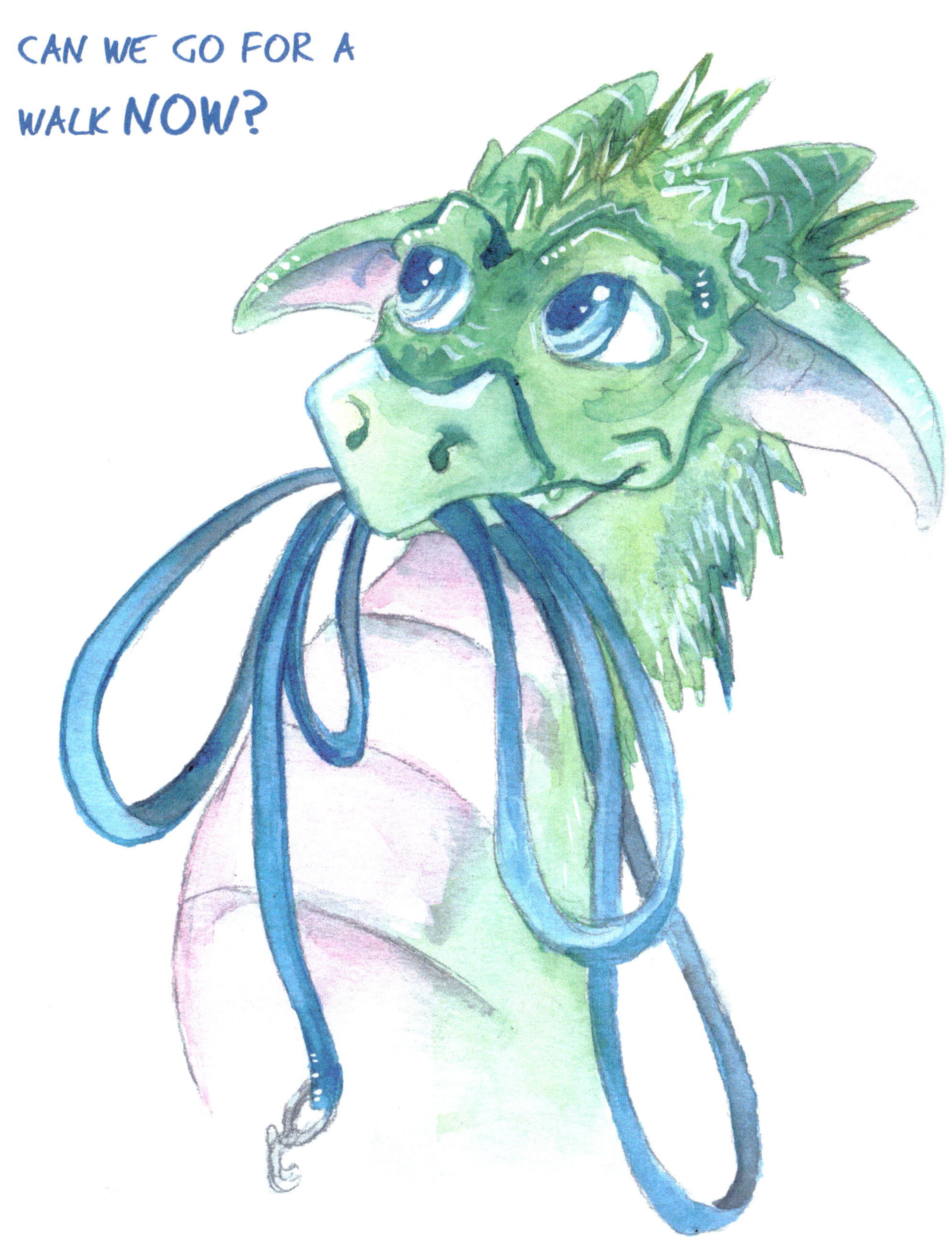

Painting Feathers

Here are some basic techniques for painting feathers that can be used when painting feathered dragons:

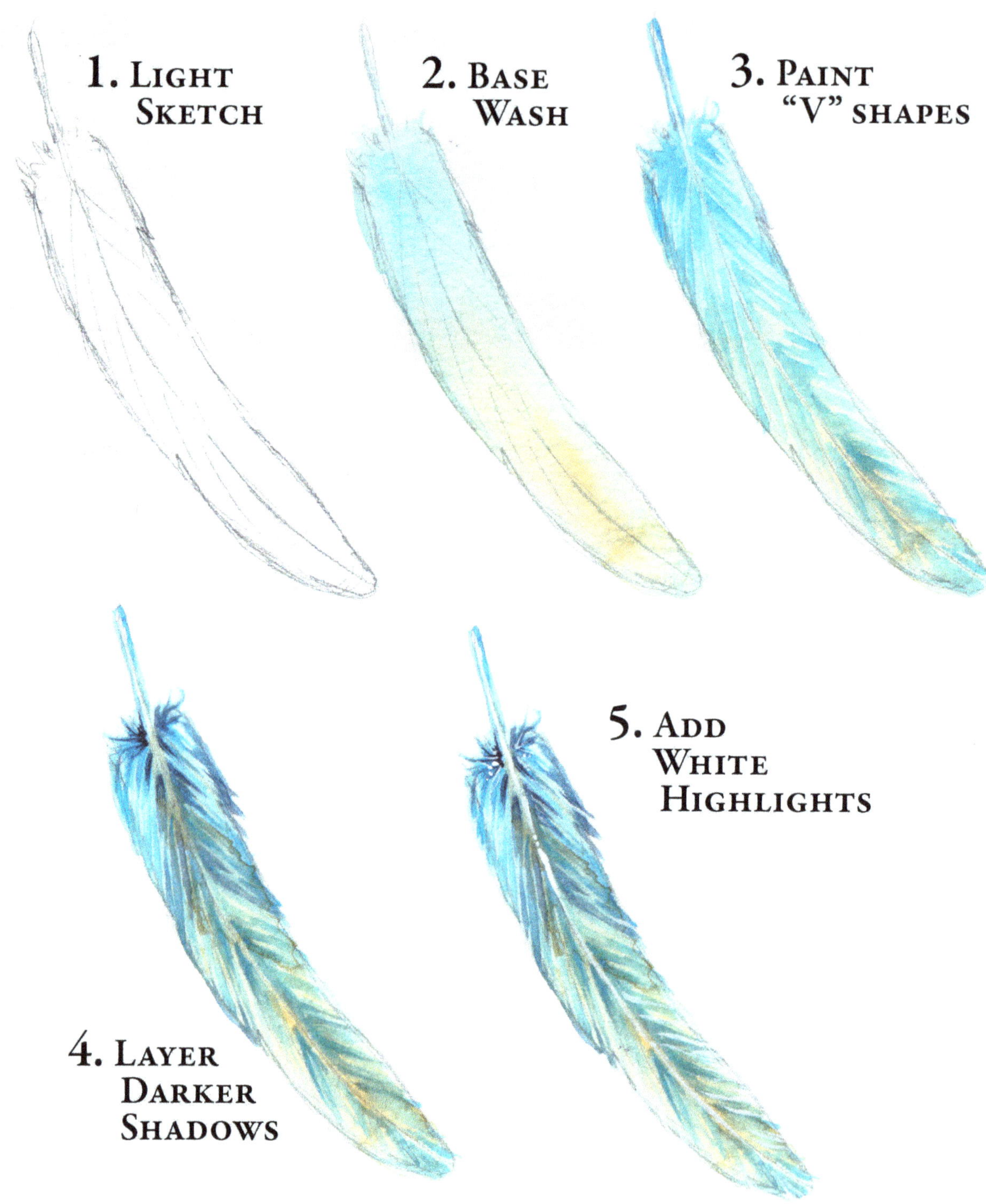

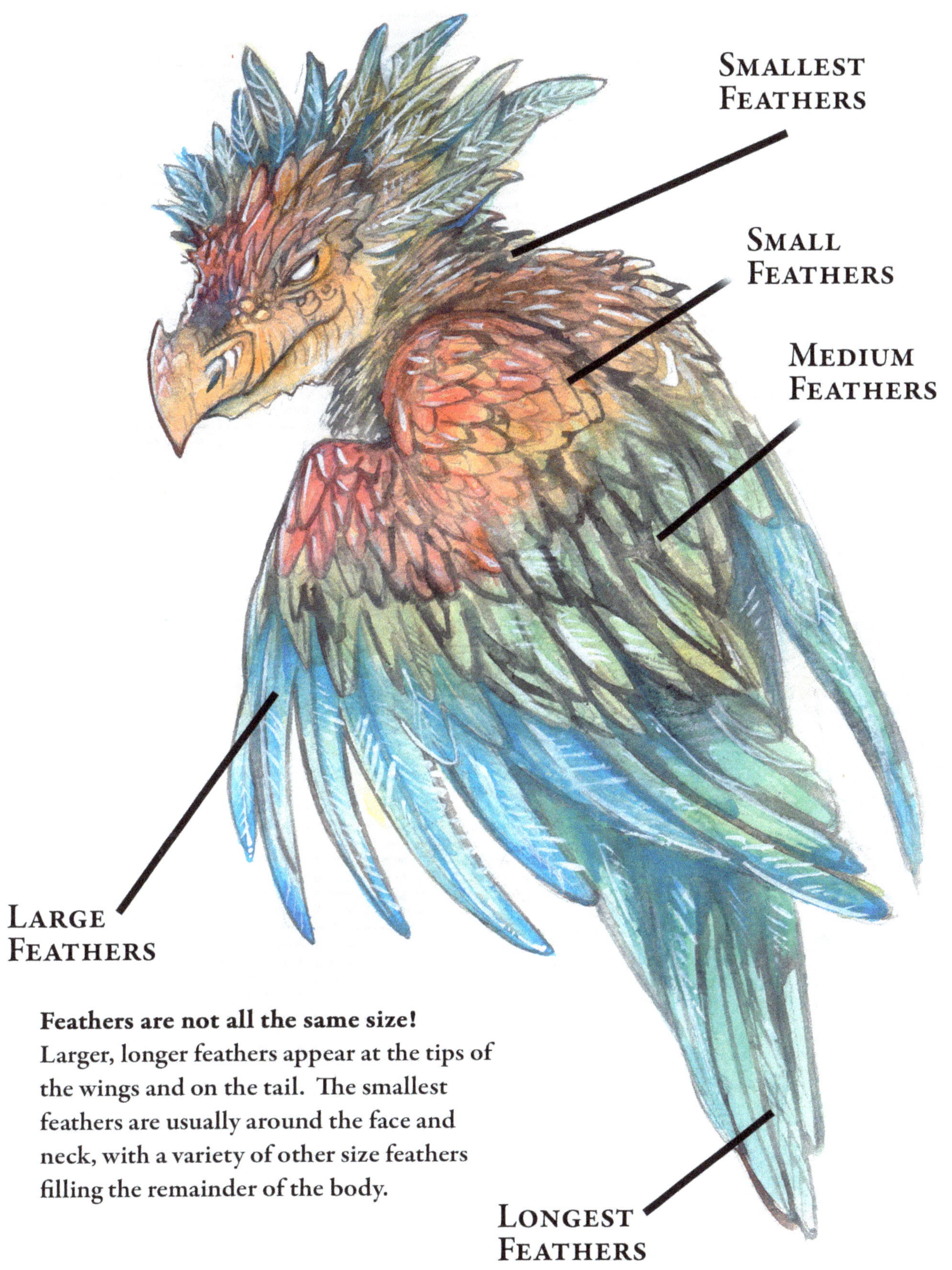

Feathers are not all the same size! Larger, longer feathers appear at the tips of the wings and on the tail. The smallest feathers are usually around the face and neck, with a variety of other size feathers filling the remainder of the body.

Feather Dragon

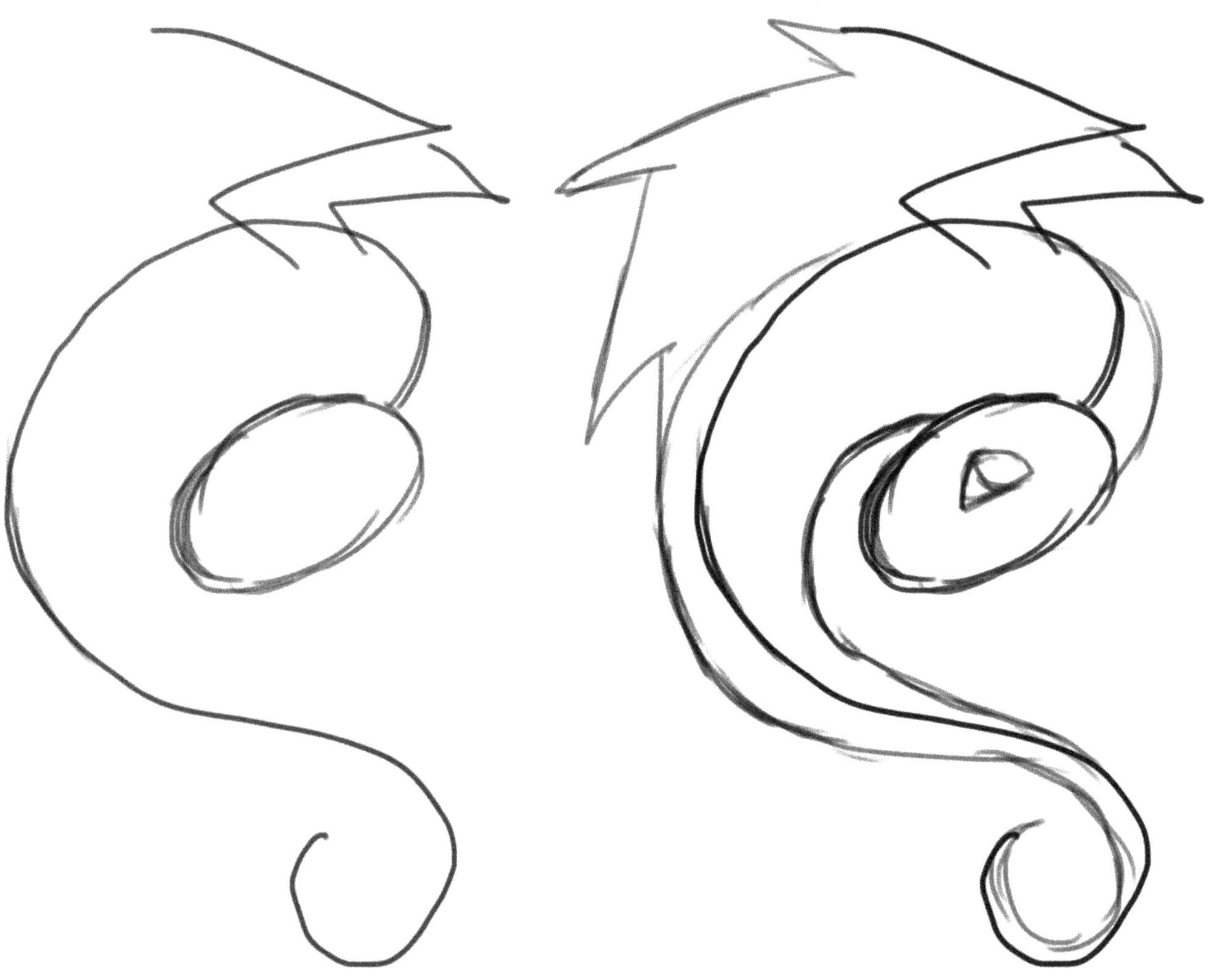

1. Place the head, body, and wings

Start with an oval shape for the head and then a curved center line for the body. Next place two letter "Z" shapes for the base of the wings.

2. Basic Shapes

Now place basic shapes for the body around the center line you already drew. Continue the closer wing shape using more zig zags. Don't forget to place the eye on the head too!

3. Rough in Details

Now you can rough in the details planning a beak-like face and feathers.

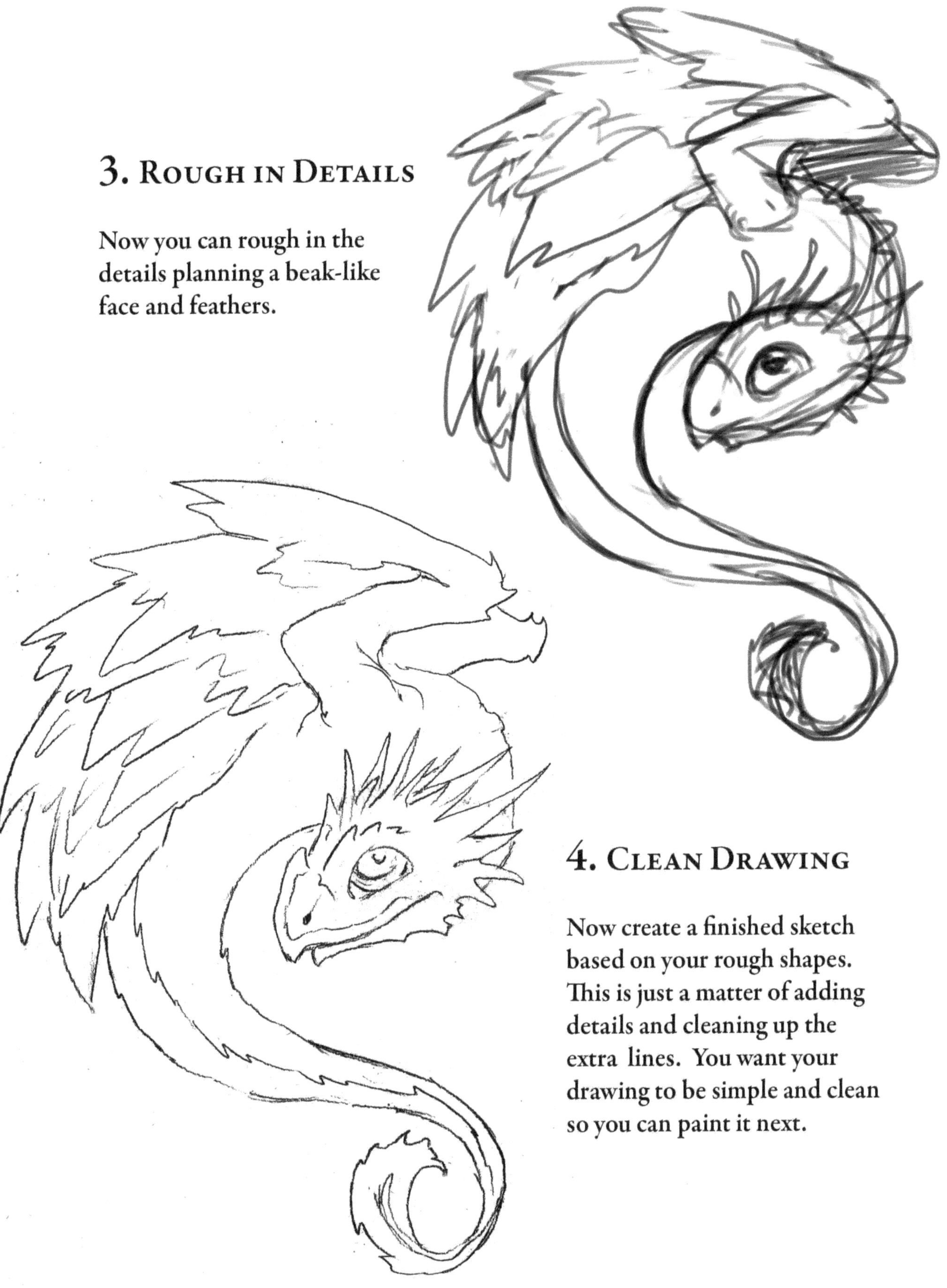

4. Clean Drawing

Now create a finished sketch based on your rough shapes. This is just a matter of adding details and cleaning up the extra lines. You want your drawing to be simple and clean so you can paint it next.

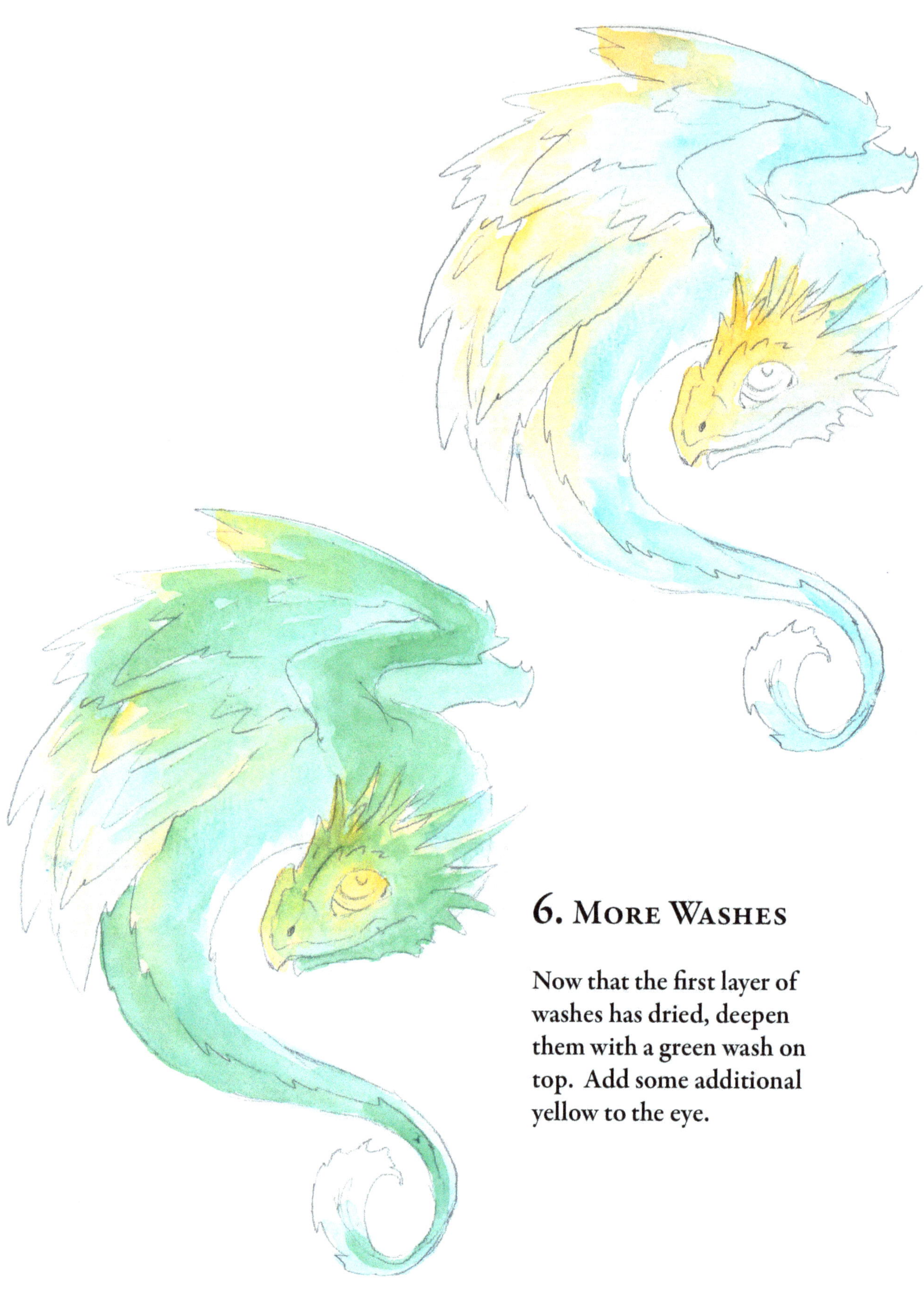

6. More Washes

Now that the first layer of washes has dried, deepen them with a green wash on top. Add some additional yellow to the eye.

7. Deeper Shadows

Using a smaller brush and more green darken the shadows for the feathers and on the face. Once this has dried use some yellow and orange for the tips of the feathers and eye.

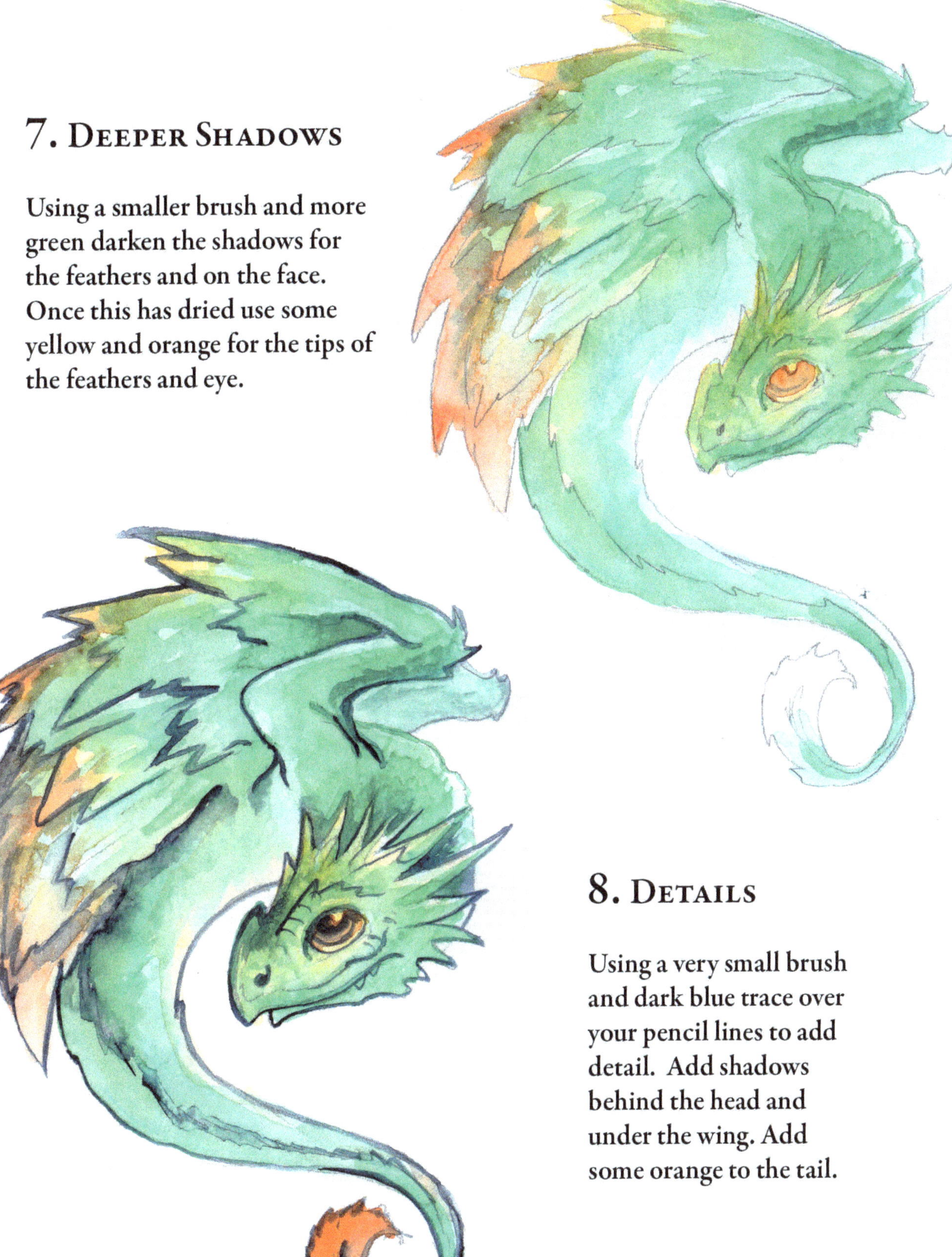

8. Details

Using a very small brush and dark blue trace over your pencil lines to add detail. Add shadows behind the head and under the wing. Add some orange to the tail.

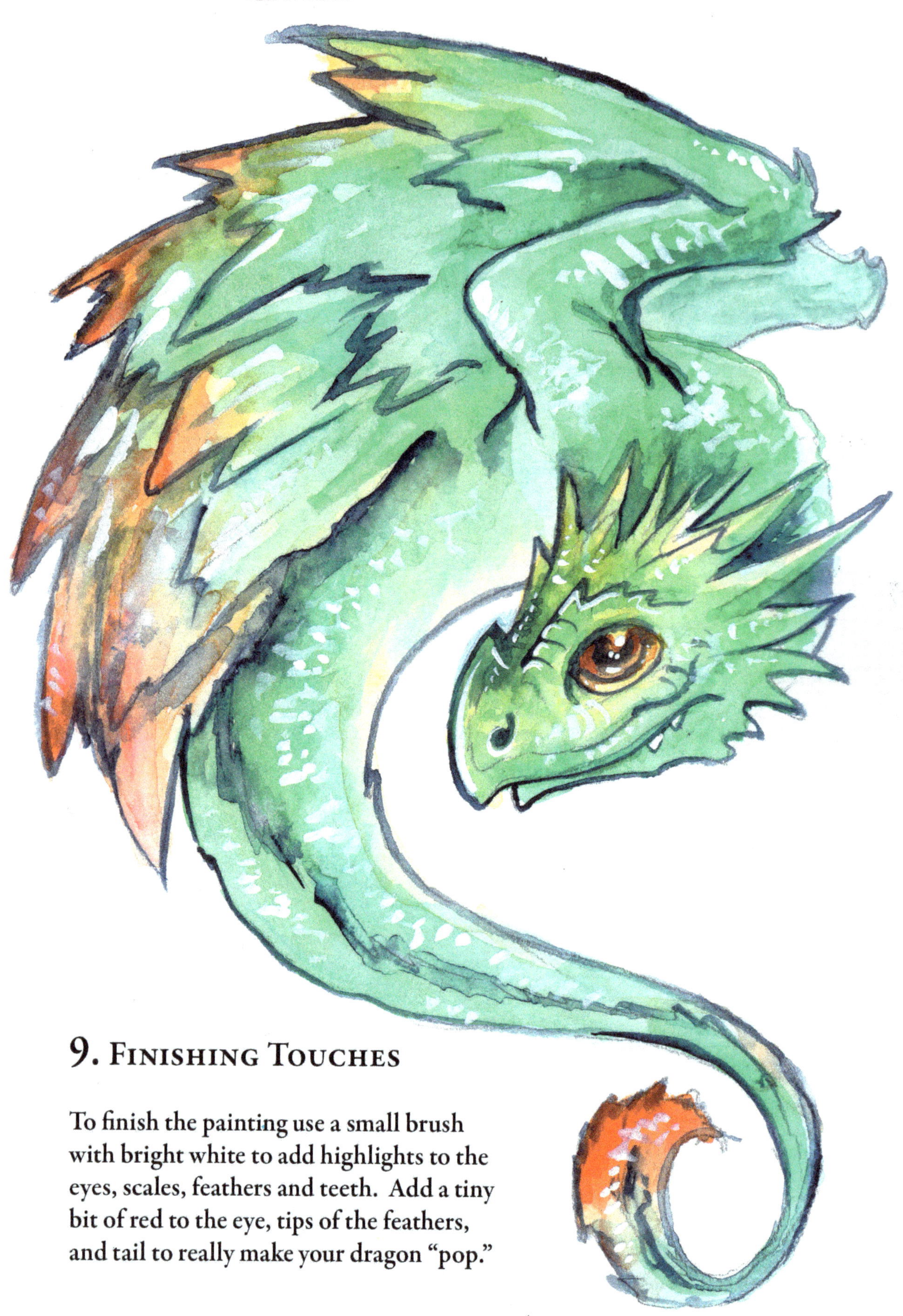

9. Finishing Touches

To finish the painting use a small brush with bright white to add highlights to the eyes, scales, feathers and teeth. Add a tiny bit of red to the eye, tips of the feathers, and tail to really make your dragon "pop."

Seahorse Dragon

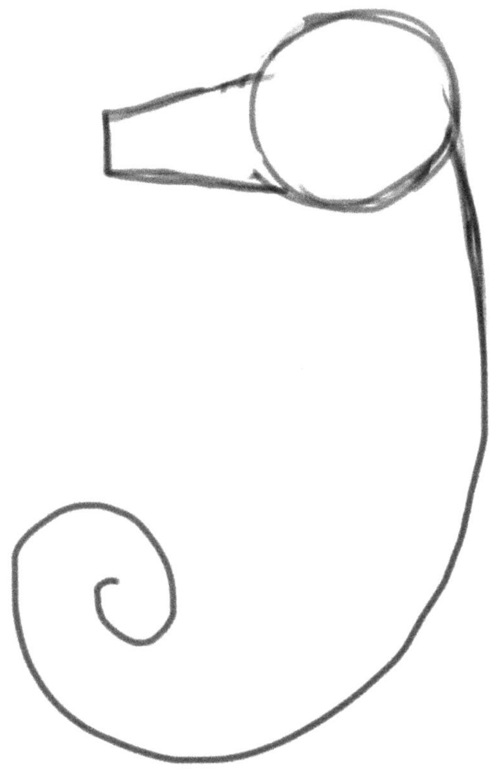

1. Head & Center Line

First place basic shapes for the head and a curling center line for the body.

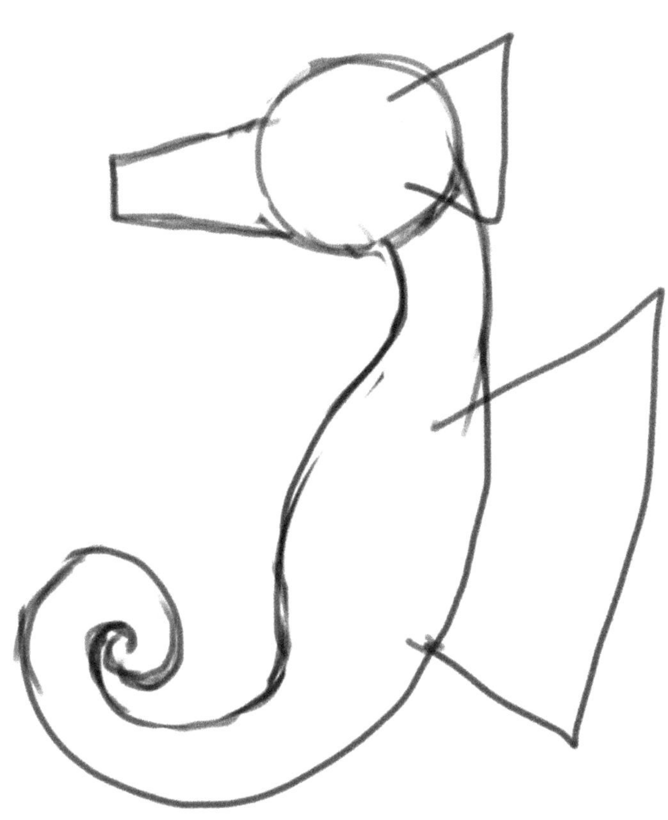

2. Block in the Body

Next use basic shapes to block in the rest of the body. This includes a fin-like ear on the head and larger flipper-fin on the body.

3. More specific shapes

Using the basic shapes draw out more refined shapes for the head and body. This includes placing the eye and making the web shapes for the fins.

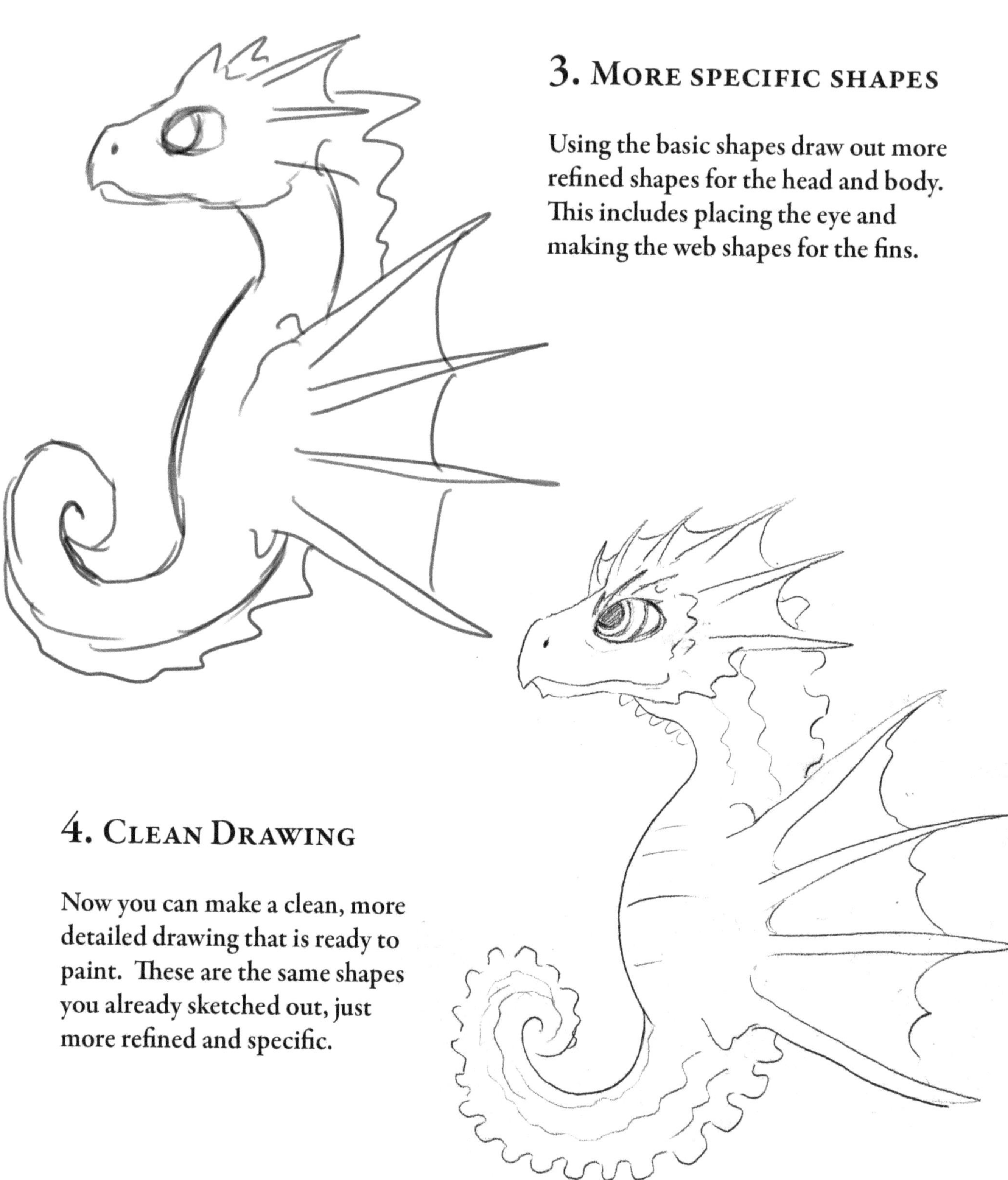

4. Clean Drawing

Now you can make a clean, more detailed drawing that is ready to paint. These are the same shapes you already sketched out, just more refined and specific.

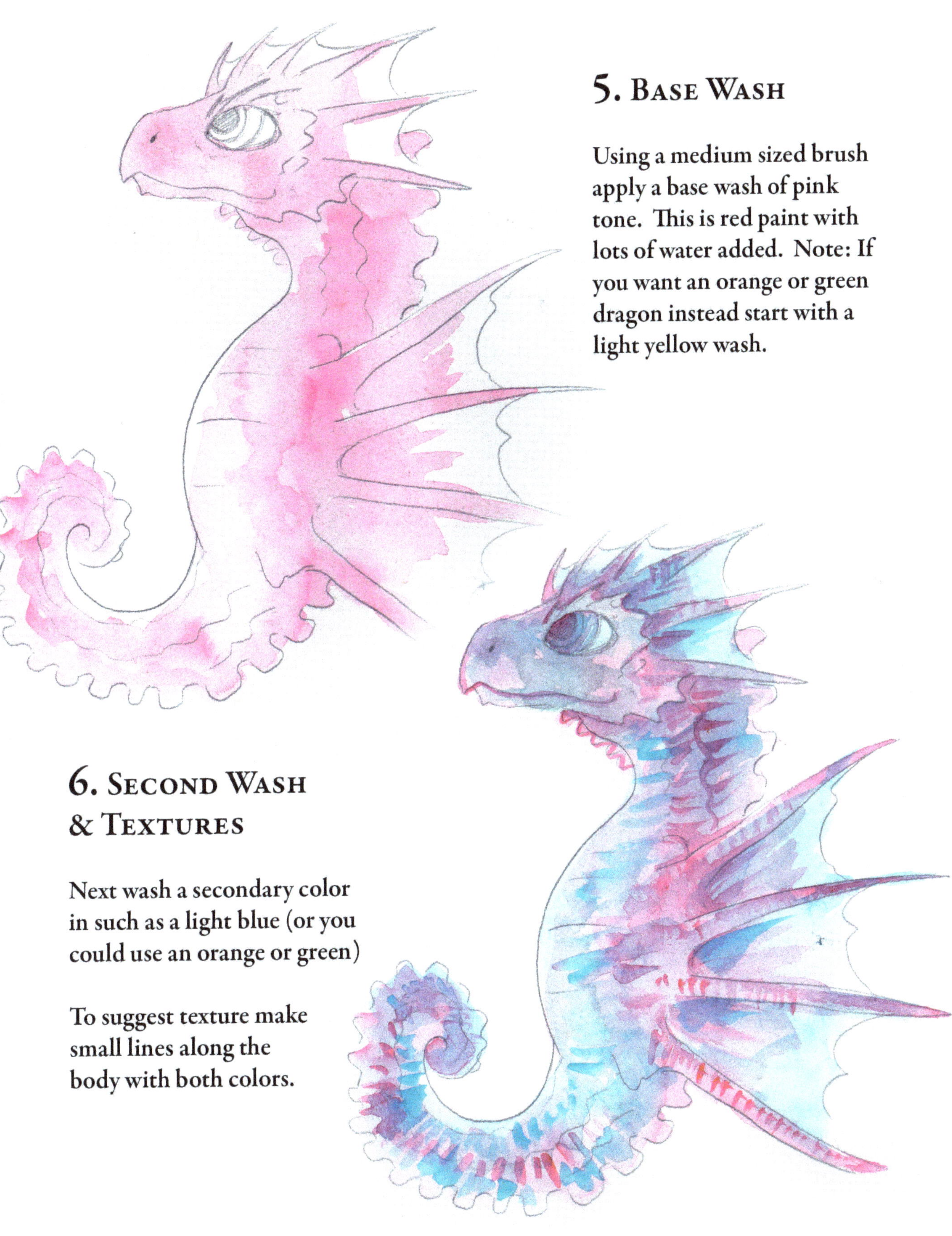

5. Base Wash

Using a medium sized brush apply a base wash of pink tone. This is red paint with lots of water added. Note: If you want an orange or green dragon instead start with a light yellow wash.

6. Second Wash & Textures

Next wash a secondary color in such as a light blue (or you could use an orange or green)

To suggest texture make small lines along the body with both colors.

7. Highlights

To finish up just add some white highlights to the eyes and body to make the dragon have shiny scales.

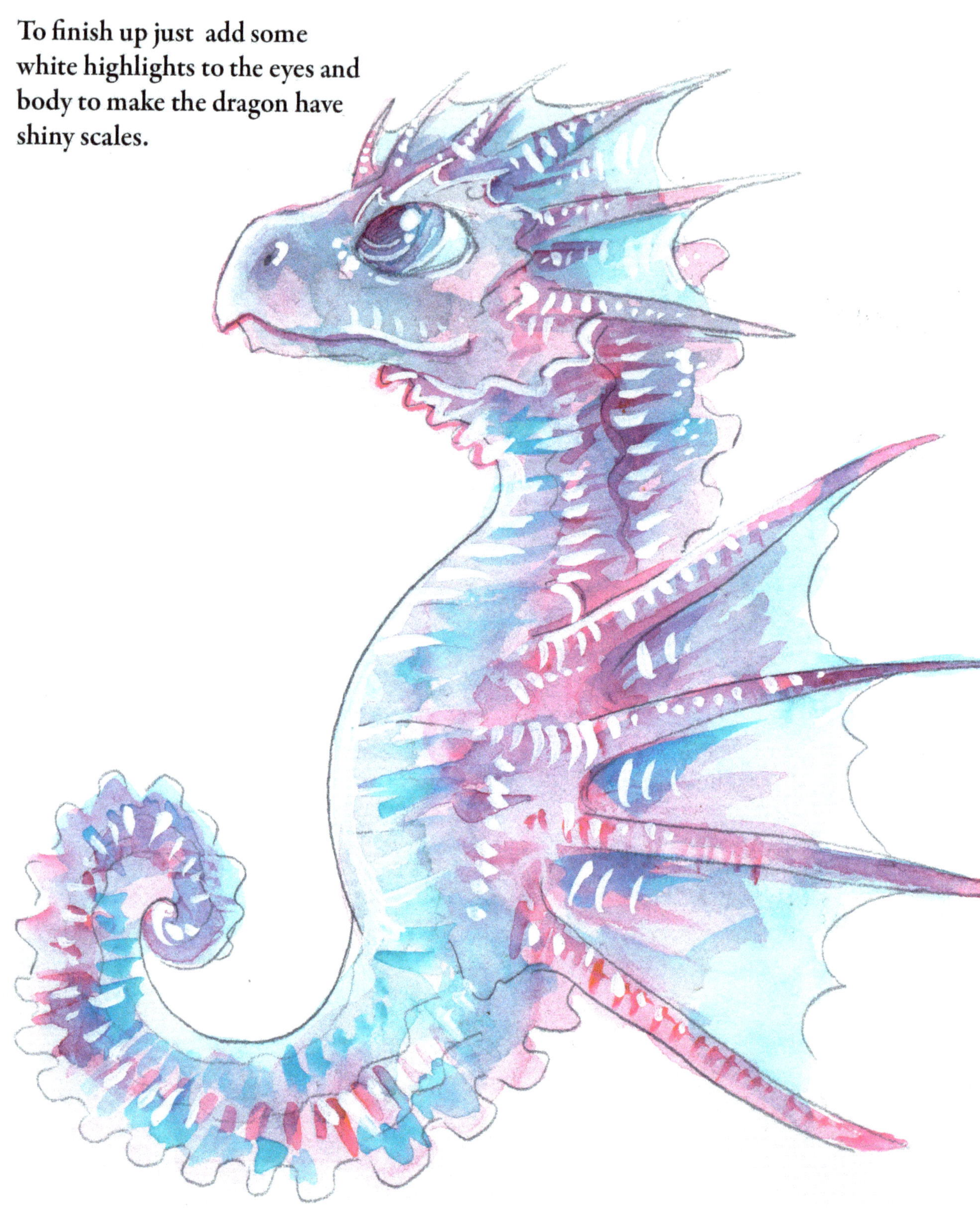

Yummy Worms!

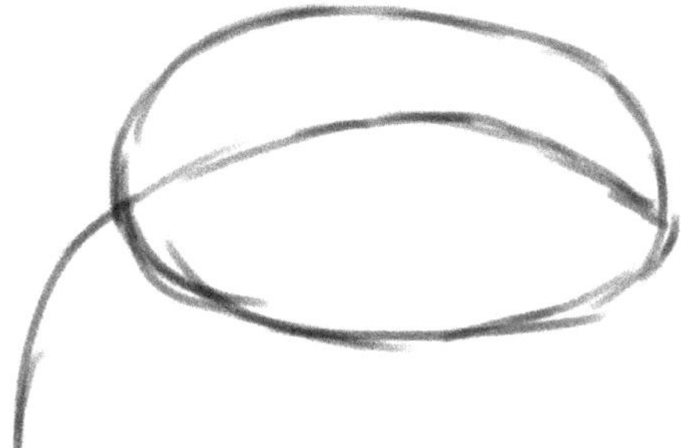

1. Head Placement

Place an oval for the head and a curved center line through it where the body will go.

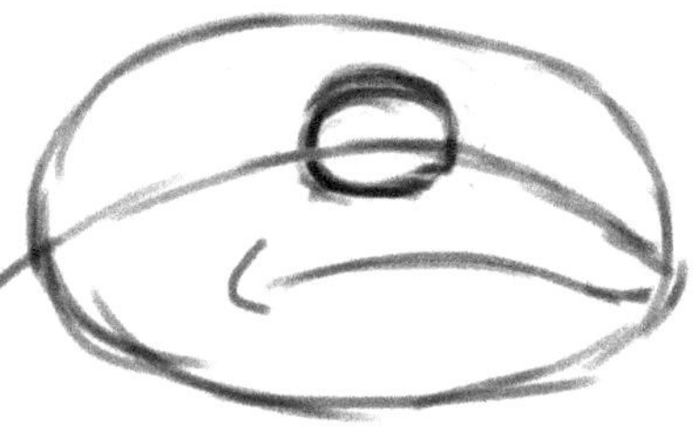

2. Eye & Mouth

Draw a small circle on the center line to place the eye and a slightly curved arrow shape for the mouth.

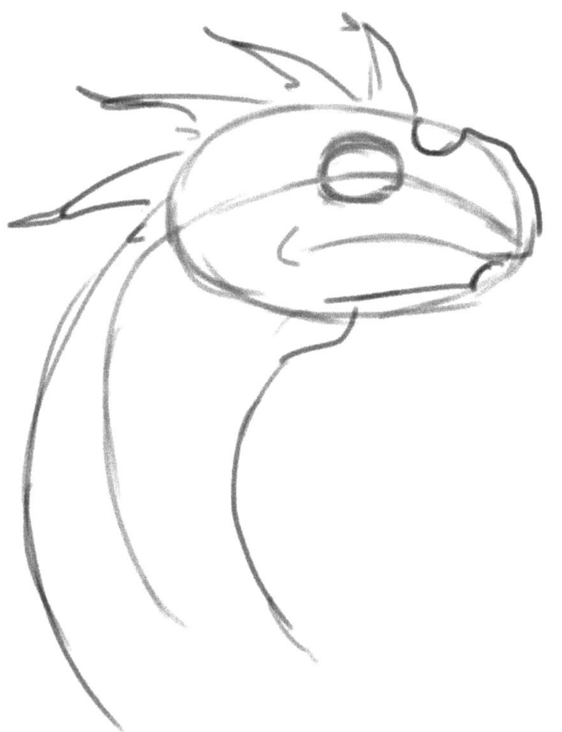

3. Refine the shapes

Now create a "C" shaped dip into your oval at the top and use that to place the nose and chin. Add some spikes to the back of the head and sketch in the body around your center line.

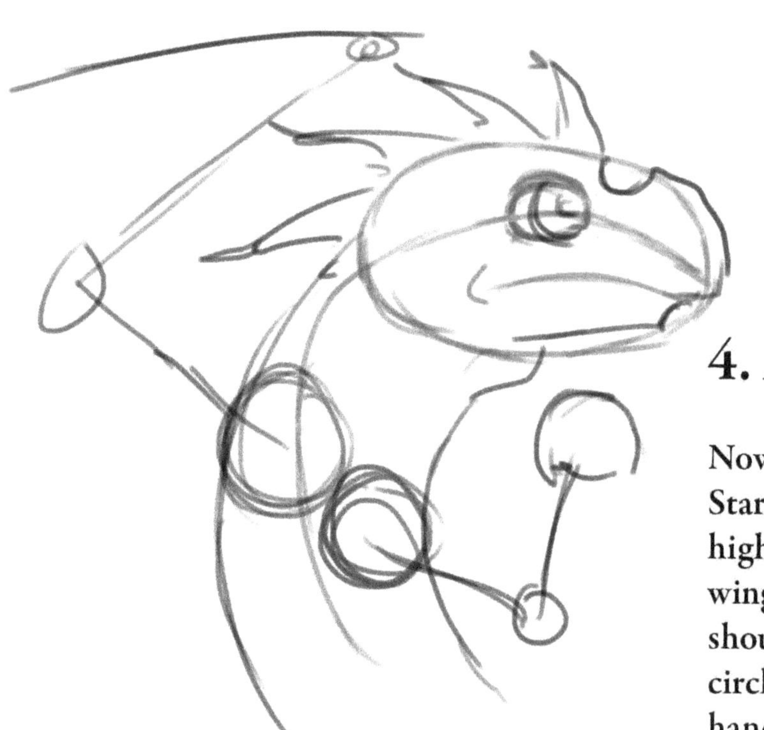

4. Adding Limbs

Now you can place in the arm and wing! Start with two circles on the body. The higher one in the back is the base of the wing, the lower one in the front is the shoulder for the arm. Use lines and circles to place the wing, elbow and hand. Note the "Z" shape of the wing.

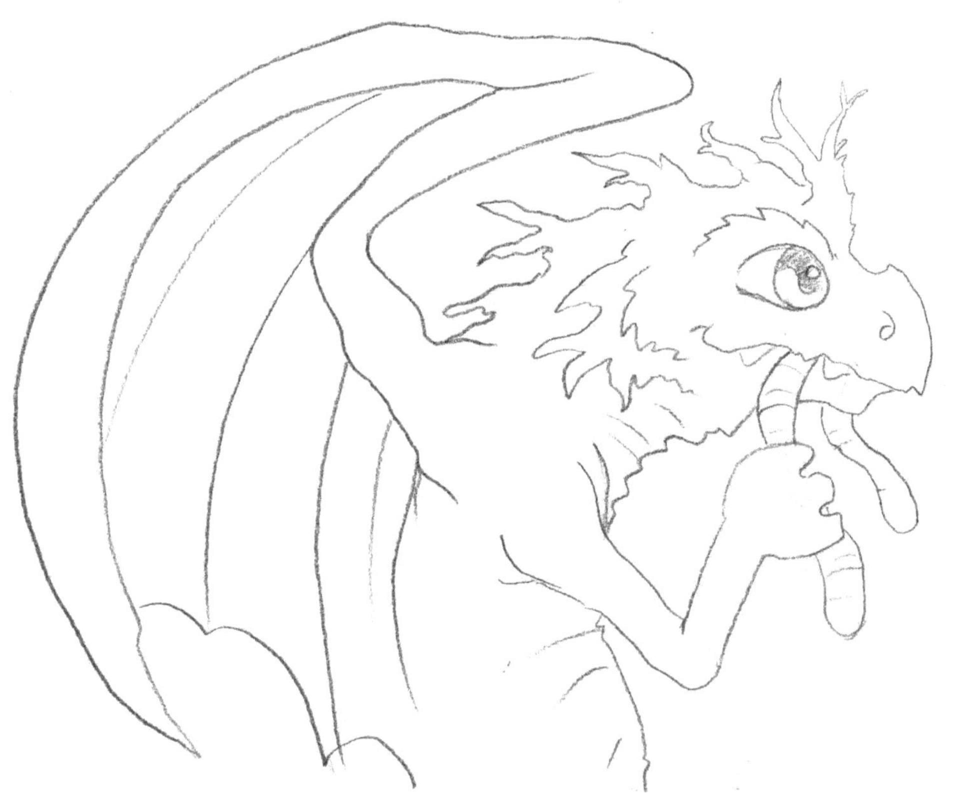

5. Drawing Details!

Now you can use your basic shapes to create a detailed drawing ready to paint! Don't forget to add the worm for him to chew on!

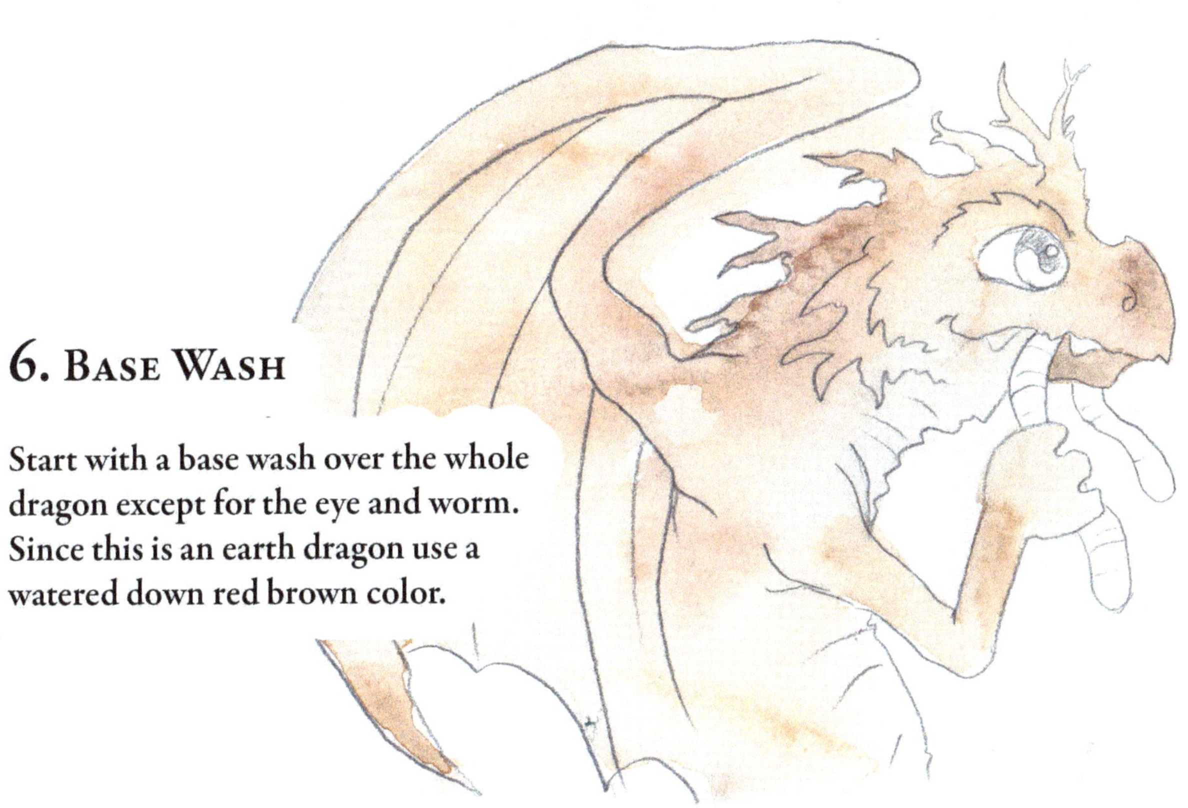

6. Base Wash

Start with a base wash over the whole dragon except for the eye and worm. Since this is an earth dragon use a watered down red brown color.

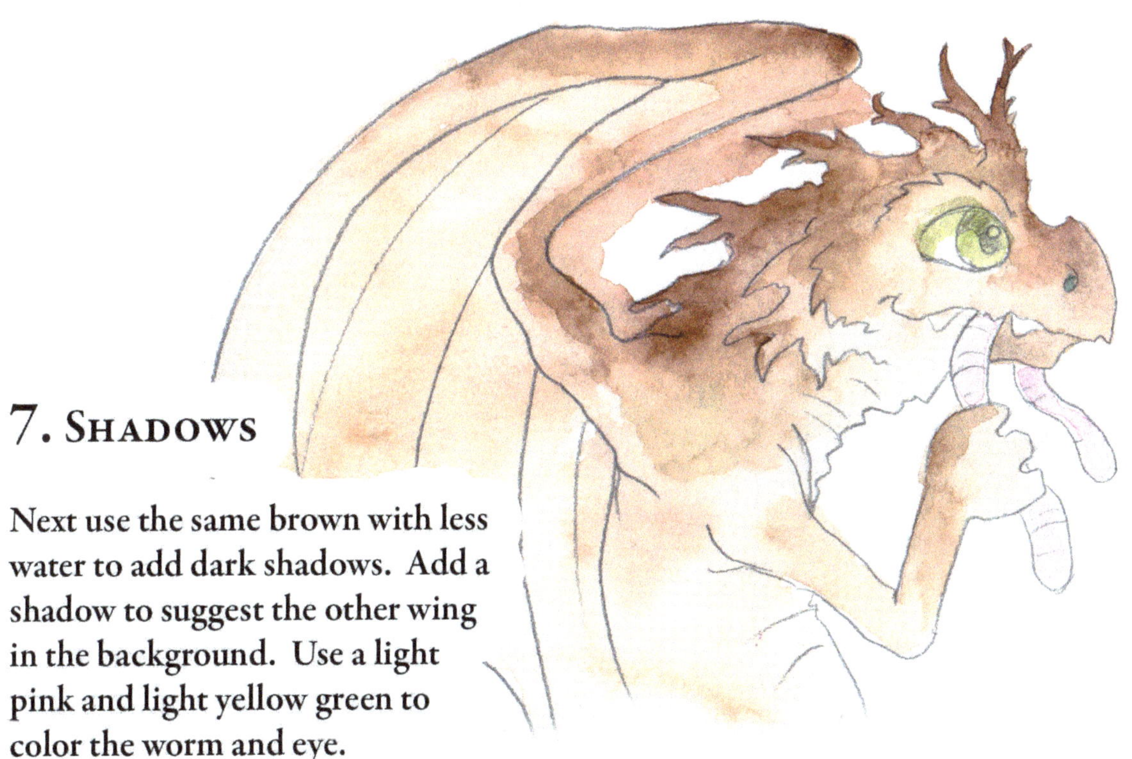

7. Shadows

Next use the same brown with less water to add dark shadows. Add a shadow to suggest the other wing in the background. Use a light pink and light yellow green to color the worm and eye.

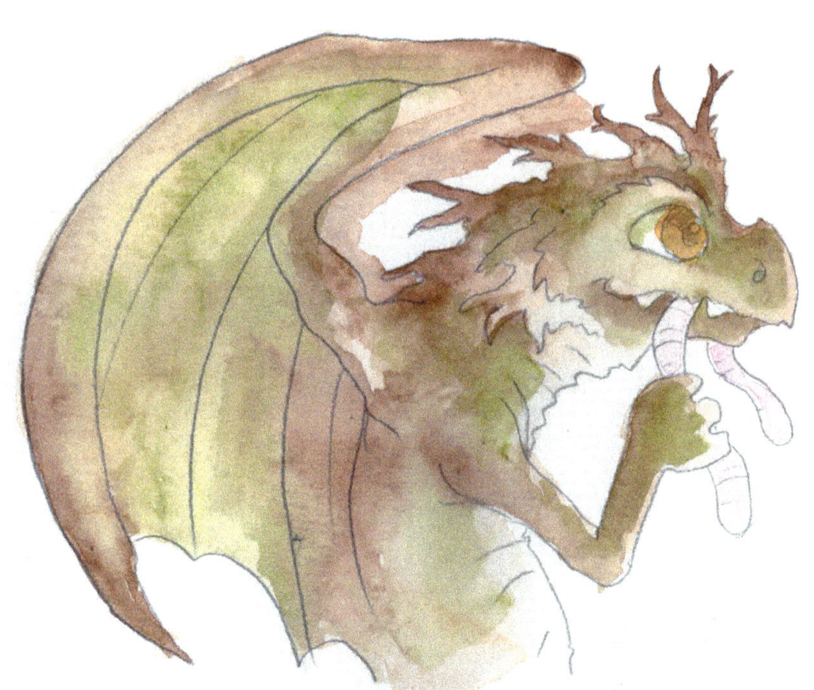

8. Second Wash

Use the same yellow green color and wash over the inside of the wing, parts of the face and body. Add yellow orange to the eye.

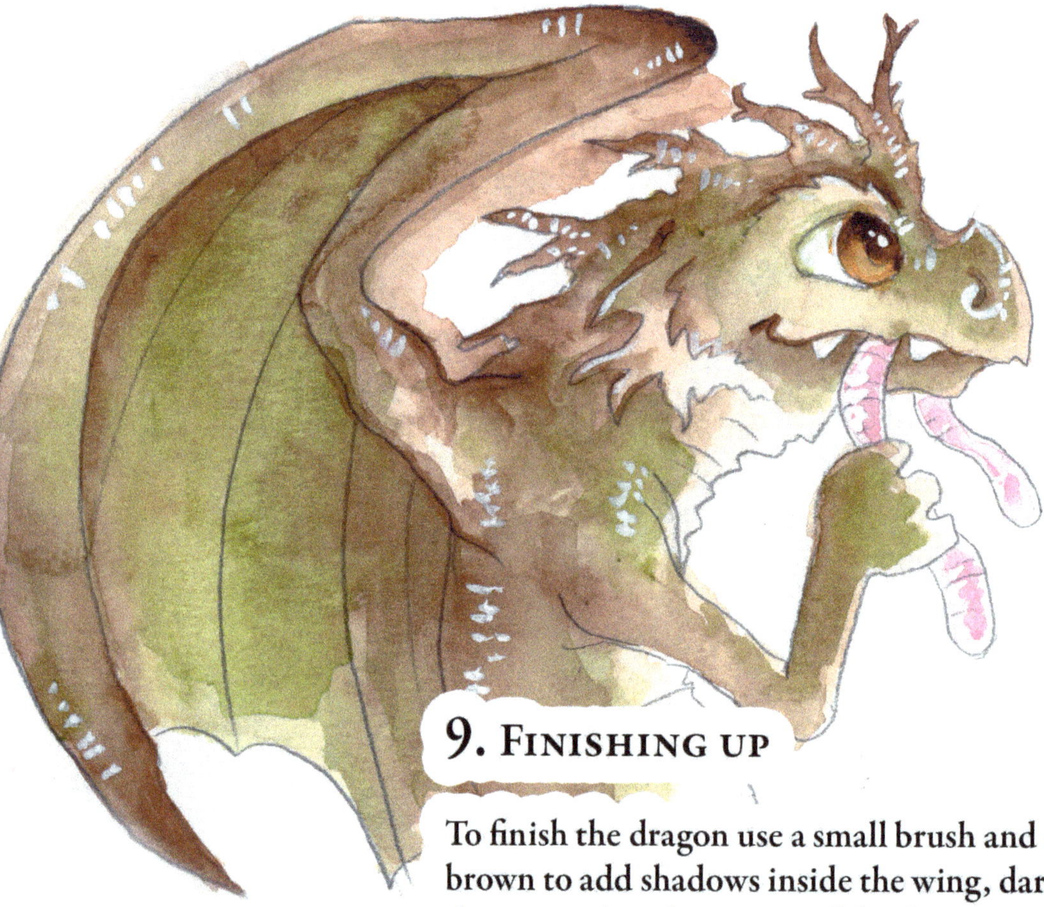

9. Finishing up

To finish the dragon use a small brush and dark brown to add shadows inside the wing, darken the eye, and outline some of the details. Once this is dry use bright white to add highlights.

Holding a pencil

1. Place the head and body

Start with an oval shape for the head and then place a line below it to figure out where the body will be. This center line helps you figure out the pose for the dragon from neck to tail.

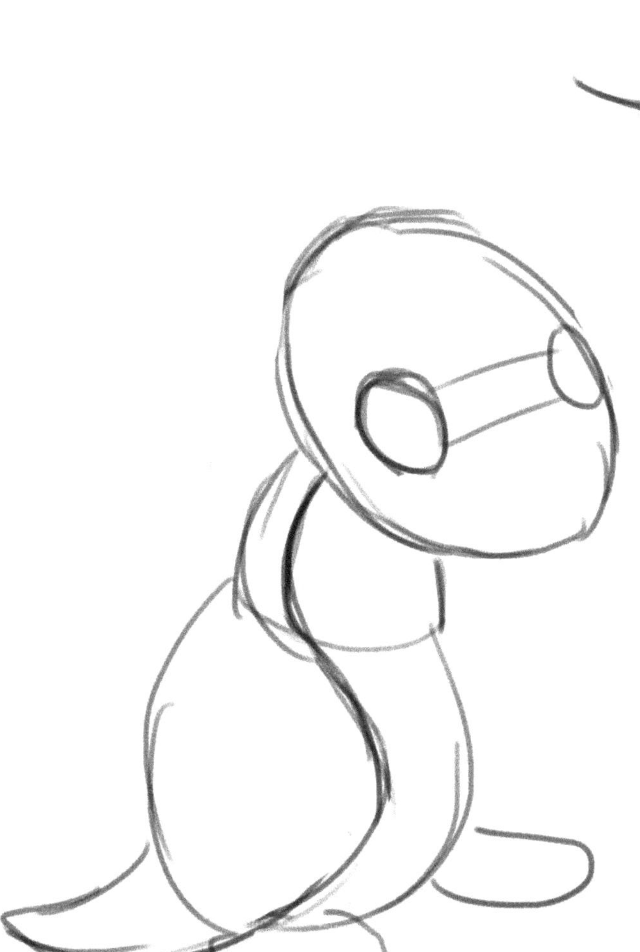

2. Basic Shapes

Now place basic shapes using the head shape and center line you already drew. In this case some ovals for the eyes (lines across help to line them up), a small chest, larger belly, tail, and an idea of where the feet will be.

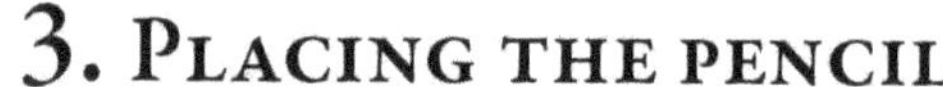

3. Placing the pencil

Placing the pencil is easy - it's a few basic shapes. Then you can put some ovals in for the hands too.

Don't forget to add some paper for him to draw on! You could also make him holding something else like a pen, paintbrush, candy cane etc. The same basic shapes apply.

4. Clean Drawing

Using the basic shapes as a guide, create a finished sketch. This is just a matter of adding details to the pencil, some spikes to the back of the dragon, plus refining the shapes for his limbs.

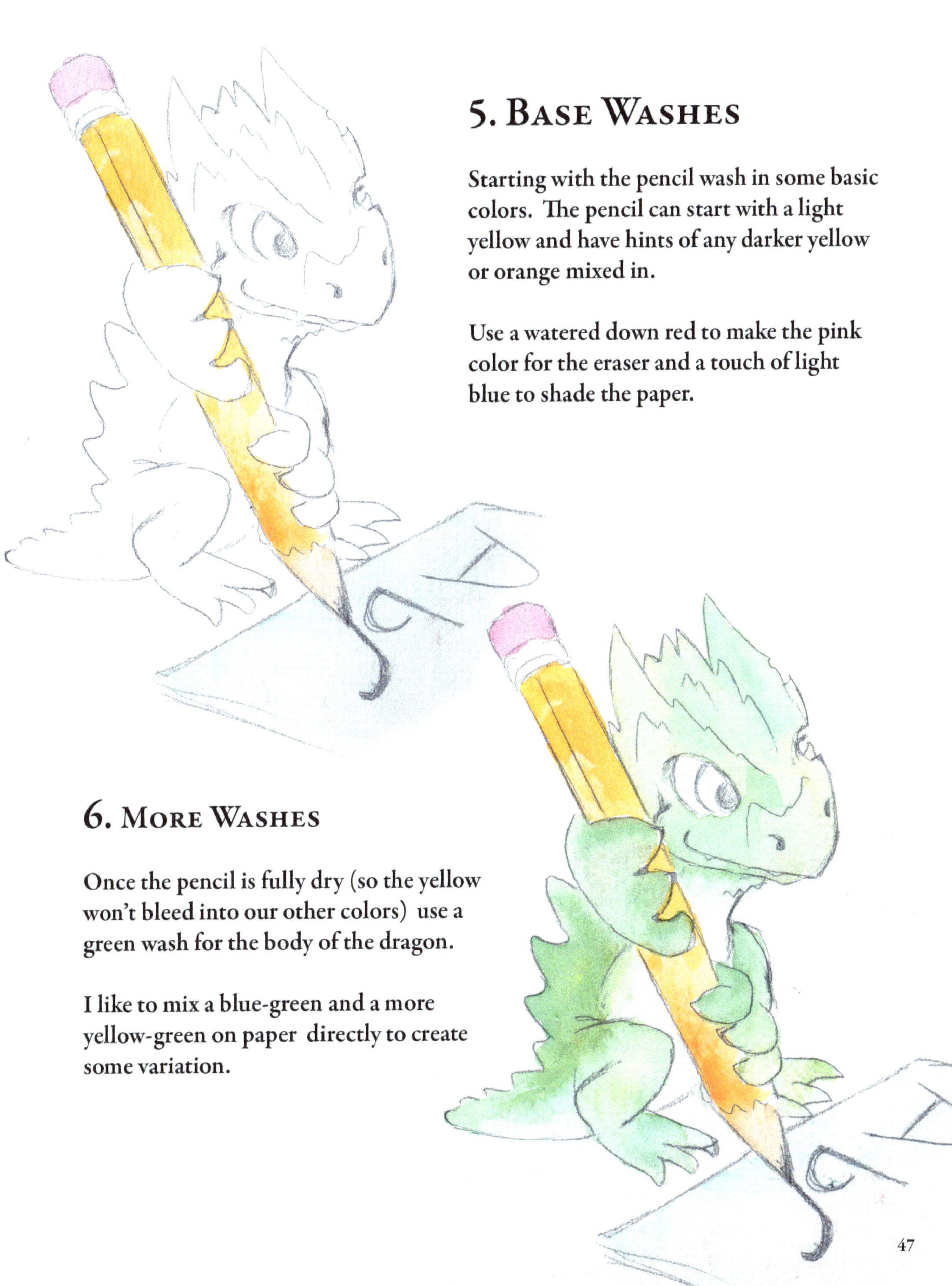

5. Base Washes

Starting with the pencil wash in some basic colors. The pencil can start with a light yellow and have hints of any darker yellow or orange mixed in.

Use a watered down red to make the pink color for the eraser and a touch of light blue to shade the paper.

6. More Washes

Once the pencil is fully dry (so the yellow won't bleed into our other colors) use a green wash for the body of the dragon.

I like to mix a blue-green and a more yellow-green on paper directly to create some variation.

7. Deeper Shadows

Once the washes have dried add in some purple for the tummy and eye. Adding a touch of blue to the eye while the purple is wet will make the color pop more.

With a smaller brush add more shadows and details to the green parts of the dragon.

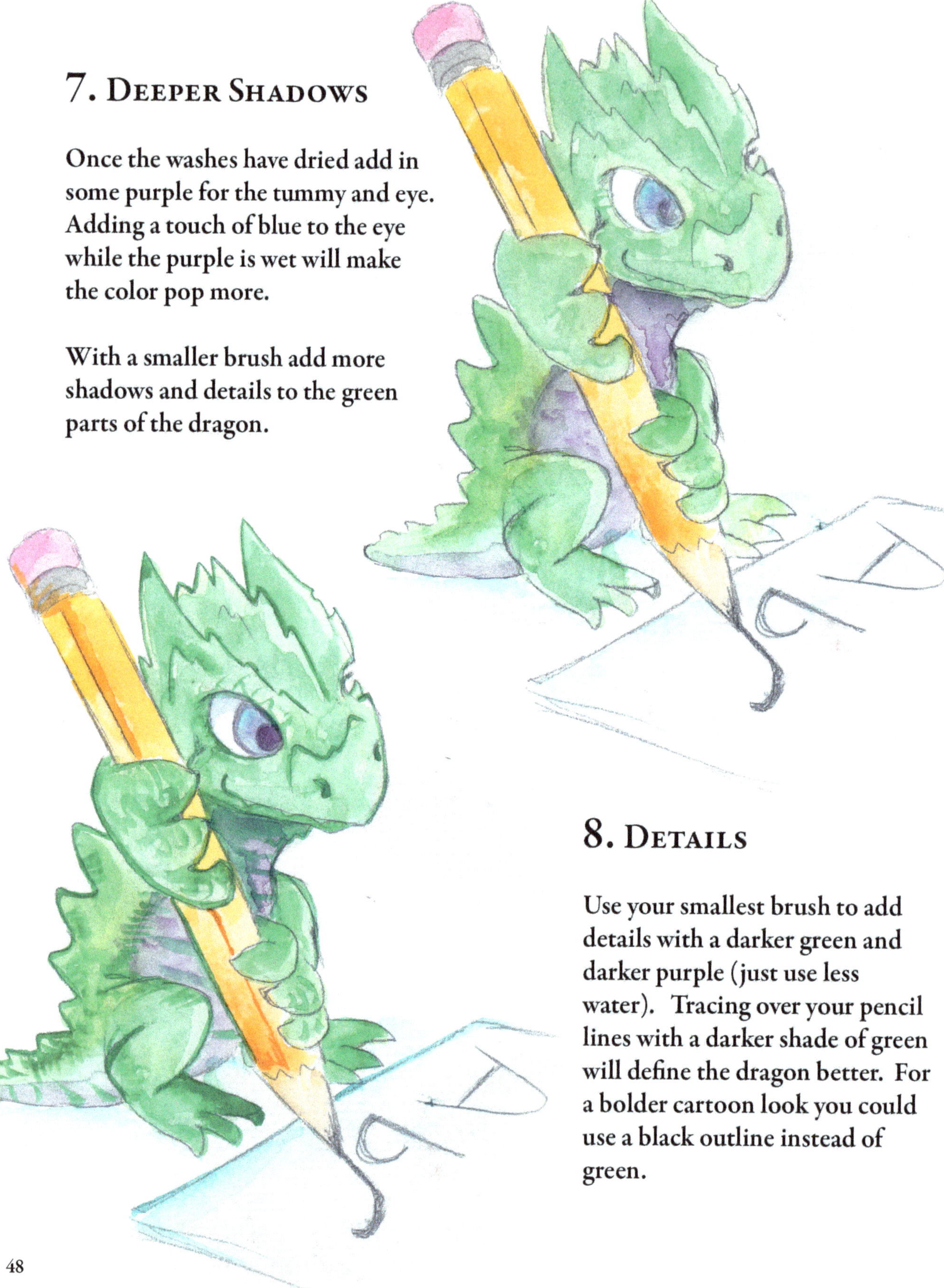

8. Details

Use your smallest brush to add details with a darker green and darker purple (just use less water). Tracing over your pencil lines with a darker shade of green will define the dragon better. For a bolder cartoon look you could use a black outline instead of green.

THANK YOU FOR READING
HOW TO DRAW & PAINT BABY DRAGONS!

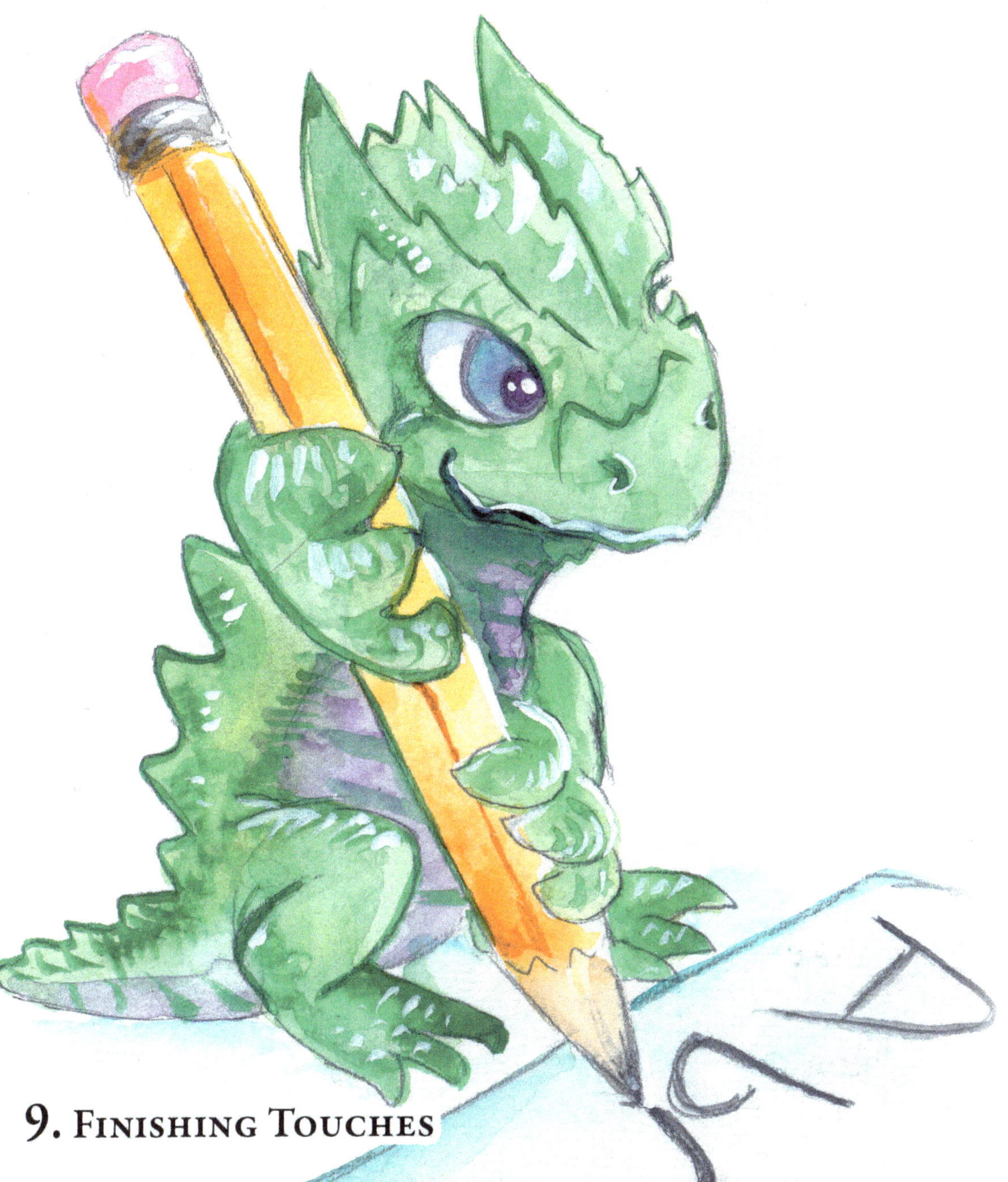

9. Finishing Touches

To finish the painting use a small brush with bright white paint or ink to add highlights to the eyes and anywhere else you think would help the painting "pop" more. This can be used to suggest scales on the body.

About the Author

Jessica Cathryn Feinberg is a driven, quirky, creative gal who resides in Tucson, Arizona with a house full of books, cats, dragons and art supplies.

From a young age, Jessica has been writing, drawing, painting, and following in the footsteps of faeries, dragons, and other mysterious creatures.

She is best known for her dragon, clockwork, and wildlife artwork as well as her field guides to rare creatures.

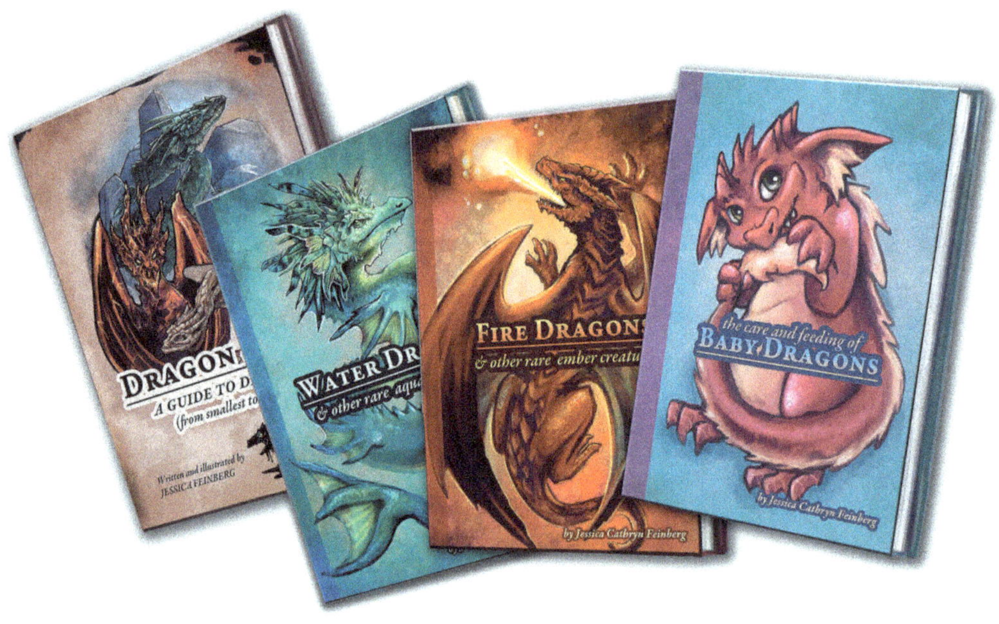

You can meet Jessica at many southwest events!
For more information visit Artlair.com

www.ingramcontent.com/pod-product-compliance
Ingram Content Group UK Ltd.
Pitfield, Milton Keynes, MK11 3LW, UK
UKHW062006290726
14090UKWH00022B/1423

9 781942 845881